Traits & Emotions

of a

SALVAGEABLE SOUL

volume II

Keeshawn Crawford

Copyright © 2022 by Keeshawn Crawford

All rights reserved. No part of this book may be reproduced or used in any manner without written permission of the copyright owner except for the use of quotations in a book review.

First paperback edition August 2022.

Dedication

To my wonderful wife, La'Shanda, who honorably makes a way for me to exhibit my creativity;

To my sister, Jamie, whose excitement to see me triumph is truly humbling;

And JoAnne, Vaughn, Louise, Yellow Bike Press (family), I am, and will forever be appreciative for your generosity and positive energy that encourages me to pursue history.

> *It is chiefly through books that we enjoy intercourse with superior minds. In the best books, great men talk to us, give us their souls into ours. God be thanked for books. They are the voices of the distant and the dead, and make us the heirs of the spiritual life of past ages. Books are the true levelers. They give to all who faithfully use them, the society, the spiritual presence of the best and greatest of our race.*
>
> —**William Ellery Channing**

Table of Contents

Preface ix

A Letter Dedicated to You xi

Lesson 1: Evolving into Maturity 15

Lesson 2: Learning to Think for Yourself 19

Lesson 3: Acquire Some Knowledge and Watch Success Appear 23

Lesson 4: The Attraction of a Good Character ... 27

Lesson 5: The Essence of a Man 33

Lesson 6: Obedience Exists in Many Forms 39

Lesson 7: Respect is the Harmony of Life 43

Lesson 8: If There Are No Opportunities, Make One 47

Lesson 9: Your Deeds Will Always Follow You ... 51

Lesson 10: Buffoons Should Never be Taken Seriously 54

Lesson 11: Accepting Responsibility for Your Actions 57

Lesson 12: Be Grateful for What You Have 60

Lesson 13: Let There Be a Purpose Behind Your Actions 65

Lesson 14: The Sight of a Hypocrite 69

Lesson 15: How Committed Are You If You Aren't Dedicated? 72

Lesson 16: Being Savvy Can Prevent You from Being Gullible 75

Lesson 17: Your Creativity Can Inspire the Next Person 78

Lesson 18: The Burden of Excuses 81

Lesson 19: Intelligence Cannot Be Seen Over the Backdrop of Stupidity 84

Lesson 20: The Nobility of a Promise 87

Lesson 21: The Sunset of Faith 90

Lesson 22: The Crippling Effects of Running the Streets 93

Lesson 23: Much Is Missed When You Are Talkative 101

Lesson 24: Desire Earnestly 104

Lesson 25: Perserverance Strengthens Your Character 108

Lesson 26: The Seeds of Our Circumstances 111

Lesson 27: The Benefits of Punctuality 116

Lesson 28: Patience Can Enhance the Fortitude of Your Character 118

Lesson 29: The Story of Lazybones 121

Lesson 30: The Importance of Good Listening 124

Lesson 31: A Quitter Could Never Become King or Queen 127

Lesson 32: The Harmony of Unity 130

Lesson 33: Good People Never Forget Kind Acts . . . 134

Lesson 34: Do Not Allow Anger to Rouse You 137

Lesson 35: The Grace of a Tranquil Mind 141

Lesson 36: The Civility of Being Tactical 144

Lesson 37: Show Them You Are Cultured 147

Lesson 38: The Art of a Good Conversation 150

Lesson 39: The Importance of Values 153

Lesson 40: The Imagination of a Visionary 156

Lesson 41: The Law of Giving and Receiving . . . 159

Lesson 42: Request Favors Only When You Need To 163

Lesson 43: It's Cool to Be Brainy 166

Lesson 44: To Win You Must Be Persistent 170

Lesson 45: It's Impossible to Win Every Battle! ... 173

Lesson 46: The Obligations of Being Responsible 177

Lesson 47: The Uncertainty of Gambling 181

Lesson 48: The Accumulation of Wealth 185

Lesson 49: The Exaggeration of Arrogance 189

Lesson 50: Be Thankful for Your Talents 192

Lesson 51: The Graciousness of Integrity 196

Lesson 52: Big Egos Hinder Our Mental Health .. 199

Lesson 53: The Best Have Failed Innumerable Times 203

Lesson 54: Don't Act Small-Mindedly 207

Lesson 55: It's Time for Change 210

Lesson 56: Be a Good Judge of Character 214

Lesson 57: Imposing on Others Isn't Good 217

Lesson 58: Use Your Head for Something Besides a Hat Rack................... 220

Lesson 59: The Scorn of Prejudice 223

Conclusion 228

Preface

Mistakes. We have all made our share of them. Some have been understandably overlooked, while others have unintentionally caused harm.

Truthfully, there was a time when my thoughts were fueled by selfishness, a lack of decency, and just plain stupidity. I insisted on pretending to be *someone* other than myself; someone who, despite knowing better, constantly refused to do so and thereby acknowledge responsibility for my actions. As a result, a niche in prison patiently awaited my arrival.

After years of wasting my life in a gloomy cell, questions of who I was and how I had arrived at such a dark place began swirling about in my mind. Sadly, I could not come up with a plausible answer, so I continued to search. In the wake of observing, reading, and listening to people as opposed to being talkative, it finally dawned on me—I had value, and I was doing all the wrong things to prove it.

Traits and Emotions of a Salvageable Soul, Vol. II is my third book. By selflessly sharing jewels that I've gathered through experience and walking amongst wise men, I thought that I might be able to hinder a few warriors from traveling down a starless road.

Life is full of possibilities. I have been blessed with a talent to write. So, who am I to shy away from this moment of opportunity to help others reach their potential? We're all good at something. But if you're not willing to help others discover their talent, how can you look down on them for acting less than they're capable of being?

If by writing this book I am only able to inspire one or two people to do better, I think God will be pleased with the sincerity of my effort. I have done my best under abnormal circumstances to make an essential contribution to society. As you will discover, not even an abode for the damned has prevented me from eloquently expressing myself with a touch of class!

— *Keeshawn Crawford*

A Letter Dedicated to You

> *If a person wants to be a part of your life, they will make an obvious effort to do so. Think twice before reserving space in your heart for people who do not make an effort to stay.*
>
> **—Anonymous**

Believe it or not, I have been where you are right now. I was forced to slow down, hit the reset button, and put things in their proper perspective. Every one of us has a unique story. Some are unbelievably heart-wrenching, while others simply lack a touch of love. No one said life would be without hardships and challenges. Perseverance, fused with a hunger to win, is what makes us special.

For a long time, you've probably been stressed out, drowning in misery, and ranting about how unfair the cards you've been dealt are. Relax—someone has arrived to set the record straight for you. Trust me, it's a pleasure to do so. Duty called upon me to step up and grab the helm. Why wouldn't I? I could never forget what it was like to be counted out, written off before developing mentally. Today is a new day. We have a brand-new deck of cards with a host who plays palms up. This letter is for you!

    Our unhinged past can no longer serve as an excuse for our sloppy performance. You are neither morally bankrupt nor psychotic. More than likely, your misfortunes came from an absence of wise counsel. Pick your head up. There is no self-pity beyond the start of this voyage. You're about to be equipped with tools that, if practiced, can help you discover your brilliancy, if indeed this is what you want. No one can make you change your bad habits. You must want to change them on your own. For starters, have faith in yourself. There are very few people who will care the way you deserve to be cared for. Learn to appreciate your personal value. You possess an ability to think, and an ambitious drive that can guide you to the galaxies. What more do you need?

    Every day you must search for a reason to make your life a quest for perfection. Protect yourself from negative influences and costly mistakes. Self-discipline is your ally. In it, you should confidently place your trust.

    Be pleasant to all. Treat people as people and always think before voicing your opinion. When the time is appropriate, allow your words to be spoken confidently.

The light has been turned on for you. It is an inspirational illumination that could prevent you from dwelling in ignorance. Take my word, it gets lonely at the bottom. Stay away from vices that will guarantee you a residency there. If you don't learn to think for yourself, someone else will take pleasure in doing it for you.

A good-hearted person would never deny you. Just be sure that you are respectful and willing to work for everything you want in life. Each morning that you are blessed to awaken, be certain to do your best to contribute something to someone, even if it is nothing more than a kind word.

Having written what I felt in my heart, I am now satisfied. After having made mistake after mistake while on my journey, I wanted to bless you with a dose of love. It's not every day that you come across someone who's willing, let alone capable of offering advice that could help you reveal your best efforts. You are all my brothers and sisters, and I feel obligated to roll out the red carpet for you. It's time for us to show the world what you are truly made of.

Love is love!

Lesson 1:

Evolving into Maturity

> Guard your tongue in youth, and in age you may mature a thought that will be of service to your people.
>
> —**Wabasha**

How can you set the standard if you are unwilling to evolve mentally, ethically, and characteristically? Where's your finesse and common decency? You no longer have a reason to use excuses. Time is generous, but it quickly flees from the fool who is without concern for how it may have been utilized. When we make up our mind and decide that it's time to grow up, then people will begin to show respect for the way we carry ourselves.

Evolving into maturity means displaying manners that are tasteful. It is also showing a mental disposition of alluring wisdom. Let's face it, growth is about allowing our personal style to exist in a more refined way; a way that permits our aura to attract those who are sincerely complementary of us.

Maturity not only plays a role in how we approach people. It also assists us in formulating positive thoughts before reacting to situations that might cause us to look foolish. Sure, we all enjoy having a little coolness in our swagger, but remembrance shall only be given to the person who's capable of showing the world that their thoughts are more advanced than their anatomical age. One of the easiest things to do in life is to walk around looking like you belong in a diaper and a bib. You know—having an expectation that everyone is here to cater, or provide for you because you lack the will to go out and make it happen for yourself. We hear you screaming that you're stuck and frustrated, but what's the real reason? I mean, what's really at the root of what you continue to call "impossible"? Calm down and hit the reset button. That's what old-timers do. They think it out. This is how mature people operate.

Nothing that has an iota of worth will magically prevail without constant effort. Maturity does not concern itself with how young or unseasoned you are. Its only worry is that you may have blown the moment by not recognizing when it was ripe for you to act in a manner greater than yourself. To be looked upon as a mature individual, you must act as the wise act and expect to embrace the challenging responsibilities of grown folks, even when you don't feel up to it. The pleasant task of dispensing pearls of wisdom in times of need for your guidance will serve as a reminder to those who know that you indeed possess an old soul.

If you are observant, you can easily see the immature moving around you. What's sad is the fact that those who refuse to act better are the very people who pretend to be so real. Those of us who are authentic find a deficiency in the balance of our numbers because there aren't enough of us who are willing to stand up and be held accountable for our shortcomings. Being mature comes with tedious obligations and the world's praise as an acknowledgment to our righteousness.

> *If you are old enough to know better, then you are old enough to do better.*
>
> **—ZAHEED B.**

Lesson 2:

Learning to Think for Yourself

> *It is not enough to have a good mind; the main thing is to use it well.*
>
> **—René Descartes**

One of the problems with not being able to find solutions to our predicaments or ridding ourselves of an impoverished lifestyle stems from an inability to correctly apply the process of thinking. A reflection upon inadequate school curriculums pressed into the fertile minds of the youth will attest to a lack of meaningful instructions for solving pertinent questions. How is anyone to successfully evolve if they have never been introduced to the fundamentals of thinking? A false claim of understanding how to think does nothing more than accumulate a cluster of bad habits; habits that tend to translate to debilitating thoughts, and such thoughts equate to a debilitated environment.

> *A slum mind provides a slum reality.*
>
> —Anye Crawford

It is essential for us to learn how to contemplate and correctly apply its directed force. An ability to create original thoughts will dispel ignorance and enable the conceiver to emerge from the grips of despair. Before such a transition can occur, we must be certain of our ability to reason without missing essential factors. Once cultivated, thinking can provide us with a knack for reasoning and applying rationality to not only our actions, but to pressing issues. This is how we acquire the power to change our circumstances.

Clearly perceive what the problem is. Keep in

mind, sometimes the real problem won't appear until after you've collected and carefully broken down all the facts. If we embrace the ability to accurately understand the problem, half the battle will have been won!

Close inspection of things we don't always consider to be worth much can provide us with a conclusive answer, or at least place us on a path to realizing the truth. Do not allow your ignorance to deprive you of finding the solutions you're seeking.

Do not be gullible. Talk of things that are factual and stay clear of opinions. Thinkers surround themselves with an assortment of intellectuals. Could you imagine how sharp our thinking would be if we were challenged to conduct all our conversations in parables and riddles? Think of the wittiness of our comprehension. Every spoken word would have a harmonious charm, well beyond a taste for swearing. Our reasoning would evolve into something critically remarkable.

> *Thinking is the hardest work there is, which is the probable reason why so few engage in it.*
>
> —**Henry Ford**

Lesson 3:

Acquire Some Knowledge and Watch Success Appear

> *Knowledge is like a garden. If it is not cultivated, it cannot be harvested.*
>
> **—Guinean Proverb**

What can be said of this thing we call knowledge? Well, for starters, you don't have to attend some fancy college or university to be considered educated. An educated person is someone who creates opportunities with the knowledge they have obtained, but the journey of learning should begin with having knowledge of self. If you cannot enrich yourself with such vital information, you will be forever enslaved to your emotions and desires. Without having your emotions under control, you will not be able to advance beyond your mental conditions. And if you're unable to change your mental conditions, you will remain stuck in a state of despair and poverty. The most beneficial knowledge we can hope to obtain at this very moment is an understanding of our errors. We must learn to be completely honest about our shortcomings. How is it that we think we understand everyone else's flaws except our own?

The next stage must consist of reconstructing your character. This is why it's important to spend each day working to create a well-balanced state of mind. Don't be in a rush to bite off more than you can chew. It will take a lifetime of trial and tribulation. If you plan on being any good at interpreting the reality around you, it is imperative for you to learn a few things of importance. The only sure way it can happen is if you develop a strong love for the truth. The world is literally a revolving classroom embedded with lessons of different significance.

Knowledge is an essential tool that we are required to have before we can gain access to the doors of success. There can be no mental transformation without it. Sure, you will continue to grow physically, but without understanding the importance of knowing a few things, your mental growth will remain stagnant. Check it out: you can't evolve as a person if you are unable to maximize each stage of your mental transformation. How can you be ambitious, self-sufficient, or think your way through problems if you don't have knowledge? Having a reservoir of knowledge will enable you to instantaneously come up with plausible solutions. When your mind is empty, you will never have anything worth contributing to a problem.

Read every chance you get. Read books that tell stories of rags to riches; stories that describe tales of failures, determination, and a rise to success. Learn about how people have helped others overcome their personal struggles while aspiring to a triumphant ending. Study encyclopedias, world history, science, math, and geography. It's not a good look when you can't explain what galaxy our solar system is a part of (the Milky Way). Develop a curiosity for how different cultures live. Step outside of your comfort zone. Study poetry. There is eloquence and inspiration to be gained from studying poetry.

Do not be afraid to embrace the adversities that come with failing. How would we ever learn if we never made mistakes? Today you may not know because you weren't taught, but through a hunger for knowledge and persistence for understanding the truth, you will gain the experience that will help you become resourceful and tremendously creative. It's hard to contend with the man or woman who can think their way through challenges, rather than offering an emotional outburst in the name of a resolution. You must be a thinker.

Life develops in stages, as does our mind. Only through acquiring knowledge can we have a real chance at becoming refreshingly whole. Seek it and you will find yourself hungering for more. Dismiss the power of it and you may become lost forever.

> *Having knowledge without utilizing common sense makes you ignorant. What good is knowledge in the hands of a fool?*
>
> —Frank Arena

Lesson 4:

The Attraction of a Good Character

> *A good tree does not bear rotten fruit; a rotten tree does not bear good fruit. Are figs gathered from thorns, or grapes from thistles? Every tree is known by its fruit.*
>
> **—Jesus Christ**

Character is the essence of who we are. It's what we do when no one is watching. Before we can be of service to others, it is important that we have a good character. Aside from the sound of your name, nothing is more pleasant than the sight of a principled character. Anyone who has ambition for creating a good name for him or herself must first practice righteous deeds and honoring their word.

At all costs, be honest! A person who struggles with being honest should never be trusted. Discover what your values are and what it means to be ethical through practice. Never provide anyone with a reason to entertain thoughts of you being dishonest. Should it occur, your name won't be worth much. Every business transaction that you engage in will be scrutinized. Once you prove to be a shady person, people will always be less than themselves around you.

Refrain from taking things that do not belong to you. Only the immoral steal from others. There's no excuse for touching things that don't belong to you. Most people work hard for what they have. With belief in yourself, you can have nice things of your own someday. Use your intellect and the world will offer everything that you're capable of handling.

Don't tell lies. One misrepresentation turns into two, and before you realize it, you not only lose track of the initial story, but you become accustomed to lying about everything under the sun. People will intentionally avoid you and believe none of what you say. Your integrity will be like worthless mud, and then you'll become the talk of the town.

Stand clear of speaking about things that you

know very little about. It has become the norm to hear others speaking about things they have no knowledge of. Some talk to be heard, and others speak to gain attention. Do not risk being exposed for pretending to know more than you really do. Regardless of where you go in this world your word should be as good as gold. Mean what you say and say exactly what you mean. If you tell someone that you'll do something, make certain that you honor that promise.

Each day you step beyond the door of your home, make sure that your disposition is a good one; try being pleasant and inspirational to those who could use a boost. No person with good taste will want to be around you if all you do is talk about people or act like you're the only one with the weight of the world on their shoulders. You know better! You can never be a good friend to anyone if all you have on your mind is discussing what others are doing.

There are three types of hygiene: oral, physical, and mental. Take care of all three equally.

Oral

- Brush your teeth daily and remember to use dental floss. There is nothing appealing about having foul breath and food visibly stuck between your teeth.

Physical

- Regularly trim your fingernails. Keep your hands looking like those of royalty.

- Develop a love for looking neat. If you can only afford two pairs of pants and two shirts, wash them each night. There's no excuse for wearing soiled clothing.

- Keep your shoes clean. Like everything else about you, your shoes tell a tale of your character.

- Take pride in how you smell. A pleasant fragrance can invoke a smile.

Mental

- Always be on your best behavior. Anyone who knows something about people will be able to instantly identify the quality of your character through your mannerisms.

- Seek to conceal your flaws no matter what they may be. This is the utmost respect anyone can have for their character as well as those we are an example to. Someone, somewhere is always watching everything you do, whether in admiration or in search of inconsistencies.

- Have a sense of decency. Remember, everything has its limitations, and it is not meant for you to go around testing the boundaries of other's generosity or love for you. When you have been blessed to be in the company of good people, don't be a schemer who plots on their possessions, or conjures up a plan that may help you evade paying what you rightfully owe them. Entertaining such thoughts is characteristic of a snake, and people are always wary of its potential to bite.

- Mind your p's and q's, meaning: behave yourself. Avoid offending others. It is not difficult. Do what's right and refrain from doing things you know are wrong.

If your character is in harmony with the universe, it will permit you to shine almost as brightly as the sun.

> Our character is a direct reflection of the type of thoughts that we entertain.
>
> —Tyrone Dalton

Lesson 5:

The Essence of a Man

> *A boy should never expect to be treated as a man if he is unwilling to accept the responsibilities that come with being one.*
>
> —Paul A. Johnson

Shhhh. Listen for a moment. Can you hear it? The smooth melody of a jazzy tune reverberating in the depths of your soul. In honor of its authenticity, old-timers have consistently offered the inquisitive a glimpse of its charm—they called it The Essence of a Man. So esteemed were their characteristics that few people questioned the integrity of what they represented.

Today, the tides of perception have changed. America has made a sobering claim that charges men in our culture with shirking their responsibilities, refusing to care for their children and intentionally neglecting those who have given more than they had to spare. If true, how did we become so calloused? Better yet, who would have thought descendants of mighty kings, brilliant scholars, and courageous warriors would have been so uninterested in learning about those who came along before us? Our DNA is saturated with creative wisdom, untapped potential, and a resiliency that continues to inspire life. And despite that, we have still managed to embrace an attitude that lacks regard for the essence of a man.

As with the maturing of seasons, evolution entails a process of incremental growth. Likewise, boys are groomed for the stage of adolescence, and with additional cultivation, expected to evolve into responsible men. Now, as with all things tasteful, the ingredients of enlightenment require ability, education, character, and some form of distinguishable integrity. For without such enriched qualities, we are doomed to extinction! Learning how to dutifully perform the roles of a man is very honorable. It is pleasing to a woman, joyous to a child, a missed opportunity for those refusing to do better, and a serious threat to feeble males old enough to be men.

Sadly, the same pair of sandals is being used to judge every footprint found in the sand. One of the most embarrassing criticisms lodged against us is, we fail to act like adults. Another is, when angered, we have an inability to maturely express ourselves, choosing instead to lash out like a three-year-old who can't get his way. To such biased charges I respectfully beg to differ. Since it is I who has been called upon to account for our shortcomings, I would like to put forth a premise that draws a correlation between our behavior and the lack of fathers, mentors and role models in our communities who have impressionable attributes such as: values, commitment, temperament, and intelligence. All of which, if patiently imparted, could produce scores of disciplined men with admirable character.

Let me be clear! Under no stretch of the imagination am I suggesting that because of the absence of a patriarchal presence in our lives, we have an excuse to carry on as we do. However, I do submit that, in light of our aunts, mothers, sisters and grandmothers being systematically stuck with the task of counsel and being the disciplinarian to boys expected to become men, it has made it almost impossible for males to properly identify and incorporate the tenets and disposition of a man into our mental growth and spiritual development.

   For many of us, the teachings gained from a woman—honesty, tough love, strength to carry on despite hardships—were the closest ideas of what being a man was that we had. So, why would anyone ever contemplate diminishing a woman's tears, hard work, and countless sacrifices to raise her son to become someone she could be proud of? We wouldn't. A deep heartwarming appreciation is extended to every woman for doing her best with the limited resources she had to help foster our growth. Unfortunately, God did not intend for a woman to be responsible for teaching the opposite sex all there is to know about being a man; just as a man was not chosen to teach a young girl what she needs to know about womanhood. When a chef is absent from the kitchen, food critics will always complain about inadequate ingredients.

   Regardless of how lopsided the naysayers' critique of us is, we have a continuous obligation to play our part, do what's right and lead those who look up to us in the right direction. Just because certain folks believe we are muddled in life doesn't mean that we cannot, or should not, challenge each other to reveal our best.

If I hadn't come along, who would have pulled your coattail? Who would have taken the time to inform you that your actions aren't matching what you claim to be? It's time for us to tighten up! When one man looks bad, we should all feel his pain.

Each one of us has a story to tell, a song worthy of praise and a hidden gift waiting to shine. Yet most of us have chosen to do as little as possible to help enhance our image. What have you to say? In case the concept has eluded your grasp, the essence of a man is about having a distinction of actions, thoughts, and character. A man doesn't have to be told what to do. The instructions are within his heart. A man understands the importance of executing his responsibilities. A man knows how to conduct himself at all times. He would never leave the door open to be viewed as a clown! When a man truly comprehends the essence of who he is, and what he stands for, his soul will sing a tune that the world will honorably respect, no matter where he is.

> Even a peacock knows how to strut with an air of dignity.
>
> **—David Lee**

Lesson 6:

Obedience Exists in Many Forms

> *The terms of obedience cannot be fulfilled if you spend most of your time worrying about what other people may think of you conforming to authority.*
>
> —John Hancock

Being obedient has very little to do with passivity. That is certainly not the case when you become a conscious listener. If your listening skills have improved, then you should not have any difficulty hearing me explain this to you: Before you move from life's valleys to its prestigious mountain tops, you must learn to be obedient. You cannot act like a spoiled child who constantly complains and acts out because you can't get what you want, when you want it.

Only through a willingness to listen and comply with the instructions of those who know more than us can we advance to a higher level. Life is a full-time learning experience, which includes embracing the guidance of those who have already been where we are and done what is nothing more than a seed in our mind. Why would you want to bear the weight of being labeled functionally immature? That's what it amounts to when we cannot accept being told what to do.

There was a time when those who cared for us tried to provide guidance in the form of tough love. But of course, we never seemed able to shake the urge to have the last word. And now we are forced to reflect on what ifs and should haves. If only you would have listened!

What you need to do is wipe your tears and stop feeling bad about spilled milk. You have an opportunity to clean it up. Now, what are you going to do about your current situation? Your condition will not change until you decide to listen, follow instructions to a T and learn the importance of staying out of your own way. Obedience is discipline without feeling a need to ask any questions other than for the purpose of clarity.

Obedience Exists in Many Forms

No one enjoys being in the company of someone who's unable to pay attention and follow basic instructions. We must suppress the urge to want to be a boss before it's our time to lead. Those who are convinced that they have it all figured out, cannot be taught anything new, nor can they be shown how to do things in a more effective manner. That's something to be alarmed about.

When elders speak, listen! When someone who knows a little more than you provides you with instructions or a request, show them respect. Do as you've been asked without all the backtalk, and get rid of that awful display of arrogance you think is so becoming. It's just simple. No one is taking anything from you. Instead, they are trying to instill in you something more precious than what you had to begin with. Great people didn't become great on their own. At some point in their lives, they spent many restless days, months, and even years filled with uncertainties while accepting valuable instructions. When someone asks you to do something, it doesn't detract from who you are, it will add to the expectation of who you may become.

Not many people are able to say they've had the privilege of sitting with a sage. Cherish yours with a showing of speechless obedience. Do as you're told!

You haven't lived long enough to offer an opinion about everything. Besides, if someone wants to know what your thoughts are, they will ask you. Become acquainted with the value of being able to comply with orders, if someday you wish to dispense them. Watch your attitude so you do not risk offending those who are trying to prepare you for a meaningful position in life. You will never be able to effectively lead if you do not learn how to be obedient.

> *You cannot effectively instruct others if you have yet to learn how to follow instructions.*
>
> —Hezekiah C.

Lesson 7:

Respect is the Harmony of Life

> *One's life has value so long as one attributes value to the life of others, by means of love, friendship, indignation, and compassion.*
>
> —Simone de Beauvoir

There is nothing too big nor too small, tangible or intangible, that is unworthy of receiving respect. The laws of nature are clearly defined by uncompromising boundaries and a harmonious reality that naturally exists between everything. Respect should always be given, that is, until one's lack of manners causes offense and becomes disrespect.

Although we all are entitled to be respected, keep in mind that it can only be gained the old-fashioned way—it must be earned. Your looks, your appealing personality nor the sweetest words you can conjure up will ever gain you true regard. Respect begins with the love of self. You cannot expect others to admire you until you demonstrate that you value yourself first.

Do not be hasty to commit foolish acts for shallow praise. What good can come from that? There's no need to seek a false sense of respect from anyone, and should someone try to convince you otherwise, their nature may be tainted. Respect may be something that their soul hasn't been blessed to appreciate. Regardless of how well you treat others, certain people will not grasp the meaning of being reciprocal.

A display of respect shouldn't come with preconditions. The ingenious woman who has found herself down on her luck is just as worthy, if not more, than the CEO of a Fortune 500 company. Today she may be struggling to make ends meet, but with a dose of determination and a blessing from above, tomorrow she might reclaim her rightful position. And if you were the one who made fun of her condition, there will be nothing you can do or say except pray that she has a compassionate heart to forgive your ignorance!

Always extend the same respect to the janitor as you would to a Congresswoman. You have no way of knowing when that haggard-looking man you talked down to was someone of importance who happened to have lost his way.

Don't be like those who have waited until it became too late before showing respect and gratitude to those you claimed to have loved. It will be pointless. Emotional displays of regret and weeping amongst the deceased, who shall pay attention? Show your love, respect, and appreciation now. There are a few of us who do not realize how beautiful someone may have been until after they've been taken away with the certainty of never returning. Respect for the next man or woman should never be taken for granted.

> *True wealth is not measured by how many pennies you have in the bank; it is measured by how well you treat people.*
>
> **—Patricia A. Crawford**

Lesson 8:

If There Are No Opportunities, Make One

> *A person who misses his chance, like the monkey who misses his branch, can't be saved.*
>
> **—Indian proverb**

Opportunities have a way of favoring those who are prepared to receive them. Every now and again one may pass you by, but aside from such mishaps, it gravitates towards the person who is able to seize it when it comes along. As certain as you are reading this book, believe there are unseen laws of nature constantly at work. At some point in time, one of those laws was referred to as the Law of

Causation, which states, "Everything that occurs in life is a direct result of a cause." As it pertains to your present situation, there has been a sequential order of events that have directly led you to where you are now.

Any prosperous individual knows this law very well, because there is no doubt in their mind about how they've been able to secure success by exercising the creativity of their imagination, believing in themselves, and ambitiously working towards their goals with a positive attitude. Likewise, you must be willing to continue doing your part with faith, and when you least expect it, opportunity will provide you with all that you have been striving for. Believe in yourself and watch how things will begin to work in your favor.

What has been keeping you from recognizing your potential? When you get in a habit of thinking, your thoughts begin to evolve and yearn for greater challenges. Sometimes progress seems daunting, but if you continue to use your mind, ideas will spring up everywhere you look.

As you strive to do your very best, be sure not to allow your ambitions to entertain anything short of what you have been pursuing. There are no shortcuts when aiming towards perfection.

The laws that govern human nature and the universe do not give anyone a pass to leave the natural order of existence, create havoc and then try to get back in line, pretending as if they never abandoned their initial objective. Stay focused. It only takes a single moment of indiscretion or impatience to turn you away from what your heart knows to be correct. Once you understand the formula, opportunities can be created at will. Do not believe anything differently. Never lose sight of the fact that God tends to help those of us who take the initiative to help themselves first.

    Initially, you were probably sitting at home, stricken by distress, praying for someone to provide for you, then something miraculously sparked in your mind that caused you to have faith in yourself, and off you went in search of an opportunity that could help change your circumstances. Now life is much better, and you cannot stop smiling. *Anything in life is possible!* When you learn to think things through, as opposed to reacting emotionally, life becomes a bit easier.

Never be afraid to demonstrate your ability to be persistent when pursuing your goals.

—Ibraheem Gardner

Lesson 9:

Your Deeds Will Always Follow You

> *What do we live for if it is not to make life less difficult for each other?*
>
> —George Eliot

The quality of our thoughts and character can both be revealed through our behavior. Sadly, not all deeds have a genuine intent. Sometimes, what appears to be sincere and compassionate may be nothing more than a self-serving, hidden agenda. The deeds that we do for others should never be spoken of or completed in hopes of being rewarded. We do them because it's the right thing to do. The reward comes from that warm feeling that arises when you've helped someone to lighten their load. Be modest when accepting praise that comes from others, highlighting the good that you have done. When we glorify our actions, it robs us of humility and can cause us to appear insincere.

Make a choice to live your life in enrichment. In doing so, it becomes hopeful that maybe, one day our good deeds may eclipse many if not all of our unattractive deeds. When we do well it has a way of coming back to us. Here are a few examples of how our deeds can inspire us to strive a little bit harder every day:

- Show appreciation for what other people do for you.

- Always be honest rather than allowing your tongue to spread falsehoods.

- Make a sincere effort to regularly help others whether they're in need or not.

- Stand up for those who are unable to stand up for themselves.

These are a few things that may help enhance the

condition of our hearts. Embrace being generous because when God calls our number, there will be nothing we can take with us. Our actions, our words, and our deeds will be examined for the impact they have had on those attempting to build their lives one brick at a time.

Jewel

> When our deeds have spoken, the authenticity of our actions should be resounding.
>
> —Saffiya C.

Lesson 10:

Buffoons Should Never Be Taken Seriously

> *A stupid man's report of what a clever man says can never be accurate because he unconsciously translates what he hears into something he can understand.*
>
> —Bertrand Russell

Nobility has no chance of succeeding when being a clown seems to be the order of the day. Many people suffer from an identity crisis, and they never take a minute to reflect on the injurious acts of being a buffoon. They are content with thinking that it's normal to be amusing, all day long. Life is not a game. When striving for success, it is important to be mindful that those who take their obligations to heart have a low tolerance for people who act like a clown all the time.

It serves no constructive purpose to joke, joke, joke as if you haven't a care in the world. In fact, who will show appreciation for your character if you cannot act like you're worthy? It is not likely that you will be respected for your sensibility if you insist on playing the role of a clown.

Buffoons and liars both share a commonality: neither of them can be trusted. The former constantly finds pleasure in mimicking a playful kid, while the latter has a habit of distorting the truth. No one who takes life seriously wants anything to do with either one because they have nothing positive to contribute, and they are outright problematic. If your life consists of humor and playing games all day, when will you have time for reflecting and evaluating the progress you were supposed to have made? When a fool has found a way to breach your social perimeter, kindly excuse yourself and head for the nearest exit. If you permit them to occupy your time, be prepared to suffer the consequences that come with using poor judgment.

Leave the buffoonery to those who wish to be a clown forever, and never forget, decorum has boundaries that we must never exceed.

Lesson 11:

Accepting Responsibility for Your Actions

> *Don't be afraid of your faults.*
>
> **—Yoruba proverb**

Having the courage to embrace responsibility for your actions when you're wrong shows a consciousness of being honorable. Comfort can be found in the person who isn't afraid to admit they made a mistake or exercised poor judgment. There should never be an in-between course. When you are wrong, you are wrong.

Never dishonor your name by deflecting blame.

If you cannot accept full responsibility for your errors or those who are under your supervision, then how do you propose to win the confidence of people who may someday wish to follow in your footsteps? When blame lies at your feet, don't try to hide from it or attempt to create an excuse. Own it! It is better to admit your wrongs than it is to risk suffering a tarnished image.

Accepting responsibility for your actions can sometimes be painful, especially when consequences await. Know that the repercussions for being truthful are never as severe as they would be if you were to tell a lie. Everyone is prone to make mistakes. When it happens, make sure that you honor yourself by standing firmly next to your actions.

The window for showing poor judgment should be closed. You are a thinker now, which means it is impossible to get more out of life without demonstrating that you are more than what people see.

Accepting Responsibility for Your Actions

It is better to admit your mistakes than to suffer the consequences for failing to own up to your wrongs.

—Jazmyn C.

Lesson 12:

Be Grateful for What You Have

> *Being grateful is the first step to finding joy and satisfaction in all parts of your existence. Rejoice for each gift that you receive rather than mourn that in which you have lost.*
>
> —Moon Starcloud

Regardless of what type of cards life has dealt you, you can find an abundance of things to be grateful for. This morning you were blessed to open your eyes. Sadly, there were many people who weren't so fortunate. Perhaps you have food to eat; there are folks across the world, desperate and willing to do anything for a chance to enjoy a fraction of what you have. Can you imagine the hunger pains of a child whose only meal consists of a free school lunch? Surely you can find regard for your ability to tap into a variety of nourishing options daily.

Gratitude can be found everywhere. Look around. There are folks who do not have basic necessities. Hardship and mental disease prevent them from being able to bathe, brush their teeth, or maintain their physical appearance. Out of curiosity, what would you say to a family who is without plumbing and has grown accustomed to the stench that emerges from a tin bucket that's being utilized as their toilet? The next time you reach to flush, remember to count your blessings.

There are many people who have struggled all their lives with poor health. Take a moment to consider the weariness of having to take multiple drugs every day; drugs that are a vital necessity! Think of the desperation in a choice to end your life because you have grown tired of living in excruciating pain. To that I remind you: Be grateful for your health.

If you have a roof over your head, protecting you from the elements of nature, be thankful. No matter where you go there will always be an unfortunate soul who is without a warm, safe place to sleep. Try keeping that in mind the next time you verbalize your distaste for homeless people who occupy a cardboard box on *public property*.

The shoes on your feet may not be the best, but try telling that to someone who has no shoes at all. The humility found in "not having" can bring forth a realization of things that are important. Suddenly, your personal preference doesn't seem to be that pressing anymore, does it?

Today I listened to a story that caused me to become tearful. A churchgoer was sharing with me the woes of a young lady who grew up in foster care. Not long after she had begun, the woman paused and asked me, "Do you know what it's like to be loved unconditionally by family?"

To which I responded, "No, I'm afraid not."

"It's a beautiful thing," she continued. "The excitement of being embraced with joy and affection on a consistent basis is pretty special."

As our conversation progressed, I learned the young girl had never known what it was like to have family; you know, being surrounded by people who love you endlessly. The closest she had come to experiencing family was with kids in a foster home.

Be Grateful for What You Have

Eager to know what life was like beyond the roach-infested walls, she ran away with a man who treated her like a queen. He promised her love, something he'd never known himself. As time passed, his devotion of love transformed into a pledge of marriage with stability and a vision of them growing old until the end of time.

Months later, the king of her world turned out to be an abusive, insecure man who enjoyed the thrill of preying on young girls. In the end, all she had left was the love of her seven children, a broken heart, and a threat that forced her to take her kids and abandon the only home they had ever known. The world's greatest slouch grew tired of the family that he helped to create and hastily made accommodations for another runaway who was younger than the last one. True story!

So tell me, for a young mother who had never been taught how to be independent, can gratitude not be found in her motherly instinct to be selfless, resilient and emotionally strong? Think about it. In her rare moments of solitude, all she could think about was how to clothe, feed and find shelter for her seven babies while maintaining her strength to keep on keeping on. Now, after having read a story filled with triumph and persistence, can you not find gratitude in your personal journey? Before we can enjoy the blessings of tomorrow, we must learn to be satisfied with the gifts from today.

> *If we have yet to develop an appreciation for all that we have, it would be a wasted prayer to ask for anything in addition.*
>
> —Levin H. Mitchell

Lesson 13:

Let There Be a Purpose Behind Your Actions

> Everything on earth has a purpose; every disease has an herb to cure it; and every person a mission. This is the Indian theory of existence.
>
> —Morning Dove

Each of us exists for a special reason. Some of us have been created to showcase unique talents, fulfill certain roles, or to serve as a wellspring for untapped wisdom. Every quest for self-definition should compel you to move with a purpose. It doesn't matter whether you're mentally arranging ideas, executing a plan, or helping other people; there should always be a meaning behind your actions. Such awareness may one day prevent you from being accused of failing to be sensible or thinking before you act.

Before you make a move, ask yourself—what is the purpose? Is the cause a selfless one? Who stands to benefit? Make sure that your thoughts and actions make sense. If someone requests your assistance, it's important to understand what's being asked of you so you can thoroughly search for hidden agendas. Some people who ask for your help will have good intentions, while others will only be concerned with taking advantage of you. Your courage, your generosity, and your desire to see people win will sooner or later expose the envy festering in the hearts of those who despise you.

Have you ever given thought to the number of problems we create by failing to think before we act? It's time for us to tighten up! There are folks out there rubbing their hands together, salivating in anticipation of you failing. Do not pretend as if you've never encountered the smiling face of someone who was a hater at heart. Why can't they be genuinely happy for you? Maybe it's because of the position you occupy in life. Perhaps it's your self-confidence combined with your personality. It could even be the way that you delicately craft your words or walk your walk. The reasons may be endless, but make no mistake about it, the assumption is real. You won't always be able to immediately identify your foe; just be aware that they may be lying in wait, praying to see the moment when you've dropped the ball.

This lesson is quite simplistic: scrutinize the details of your plans. Be mindful of what you're doing and why you are doing it. We must be wise in carrying out our responsibilities. Get in the habit of exhibiting good deeds, so that the same deeds may one day return to bless you. Have a purpose for your speech as well as your actions in hopes of discovering the intention for which your tree has been firmly planted.

> Many people wander aimlessly through life without ever becoming acquainted with the beauty of their remarkable gift.
>
> —Lauren Ostrowski

Lesson 14:

The Sight of a Hypocrite

> A hypocrite is one who looks good on the outside, but the inside is full of dead men's bones.
>
> —Unknown

If you insist on teaching the way you're teaching—by the way, it's very comforting—then you must walk the walk that goes along with it. It is impossible to hold on to respect when you have a habit of doing the opposite of what you preach. With all the knowledge you possess, if you practice regularly and apply it, it will transform to invaluable pearls. But should you find yourself schooling others on the morals of doing this and that without being an example of what the straight and narrow looks like, you will be seen as a hypocrite. It is not realistic to expect others to do as you suggest if you are not doing the right thing. Confidently lead the way and allow others to decide whether you are worthy of them following in your footsteps. And always take time to self-reflect, so there is no contradiction between your speech and actions.

In continuation of enhancing your character you must be willing to assist others with discovering their hidden talents. Be encouraging. Show them how to harness their potential. Be mindful that we need someone inspirational to guide us. Offer people the same opportunities that have been offered to you. You are wise. You shouldn't have to be reminded of what not to say or do. Use your stature to assist others as opposed to encouraging them to develop crippling habits; striving each day to be an example of your advice should leave a warm feeling within. Like it or not, someone is always listening to our speech and observing our manners. Act like it!

Permit history to transcribe a tale of your greatness. For far too long, hypocrisy has been normalized. Forge a righteous path and let it be without resounding cries of contradiction.

> Consistently show the world your best and the people will never question your ability to lead them to victory.
>
> —Cheryl Crawford

Lesson 15:

How Committed Are You If You Aren't Dedicated?

> *Everyone can rise above their circumstances and achieve success if they are dedicated to and passionate about what they do.*
>
> —Nelson R. Mandela

If you truly believe that it is within your means to become a success, then you must dedicate yourself to every task you embark upon. We are quick to declare how devoted we are to our work, but as soon as we become bored or agitated by the complexity of a problem, we quit. If you want to be taken seriously in life, you must spend quality time learning to nurture those conceivable possibilities. You cannot awaken tomorrow and decide to abandon everything you were so passionate about yesterday just because it's no longer appealing. For the world to see the best in you, you must pursue your goals relentlessly. Nothing should become a hindrance. Any job, no matter what it is, if done well, shall never escape the attention of those who can coach you to something greater than you realize. If by chance you happen to receive compliments for your devotion and hard work, just remember to say, "Thank you," and maintain your composure and smile, knowing that someone recognized your potential.

 The energy you put forth to accomplish your goals is a direct reflection of your ambition, character, and self-esteem. Whenever you accept a challenge, be sure to see it through to completion. Being a quitter tells people that you are unreliable and without motivation. Those who feel passionate about what they do in life prove to be devoted, obsessed with their goals, and welcoming of knowledge that can help them become better. Like-minded people will notice your potential, and as a result they will bestow upon you wisdom that isn't readily available to everyone.

 No matter what road you choose to travel in pursuit

of your dreams, make sure that you perfect your craft with a winning personality and dedication. If while traveling it becomes necessary to collaborate on certain projects, be sure that your team members are equally committed, and understand the importance of working together as one.

Jewel

> The more passion you pour into developing ideas, the deeper your personal impression becomes in the hearts of those who are sincerely impressed.
>
> —Ma'Leah C.

Lesson 16:

Being Savvy Can Prevent You from Being Gullible

A wise fox is hard to dupe.

—Andre M. Crawford

Irrespective of our upbringing, each of us comes to the stage of life with varying levels of intellect, discernment, and sophistication. For instance, some people have been fortunate to associate and absorb wisdom from those who know a few things about life's principles, while others have had to navigate their journey absent of any guidance at all. Oftentimes a lack of having been exposed to invaluable social tools (good communication skills, being quick-witted and observant of one's surroundings) contributes to us becoming expendable pawns. In other words, to a seasoned slickster our impressionable disposition is seen as an opportunity to advance their hidden agendas.

Be mindful: every person you meet won't be real; everything that shines won't be gold; every proposition will not be profitable; nor will an abundance of promises end up being fulfilled. Life is full of actors; some good, some bad. Those who are good will take pride in showing you the right way to go. But those who are crafty by nature will not be concerned with moral standards or giving you advice that can prevent you from becoming a victim of your environment. Your inexperience will mean nothing!

Please, listen to what I am saying to you. Even if you have lived a sheltered life, it's okay. Be wise. Act responsibly and never under any circumstances be in a hurry to ingratiate yourself with those who refuse to accept you for who you are. Behind every Kool-Aid smile there is either a heart filled with authenticity or deceit; handshakes will be extended with sincerity or as a tactic to put you at ease. When

Being Savvy Can Prevent You from Being Gullible

a stranger becomes talkative, keep in mind it could be a ploy to persuade you to reveal information that may be used against you.

Having *patience* is the key to all things and all things will mature when the time is right. You have been blessed with self-worth, common sense and decency that must be protected at all costs. Learn to question what is being asked of you—does it sound plausible? What *didn't* they say? Why, of all people, were you chosen? Simply put, be aware of who you allow into your personal space. There should be nothing in this world that can persuade you to go against the law of your nature. *Don't ever be gullible for anyone!*

Jewel

> *Learn a few things and you will find amusement in the antics of those who consider themselves to be slick as oil.*
>
> —Tyrone Tate

Lesson 17:

Your Creativity Can Inspire the Next Person

> *Creativity is so delicate a flower that praise tends to make it bloom, while discouragement often nips it in the bud.*
>
> —Alex Osborn

God could not have blessed us with a more precious ability than creativity, the faculty of our potential. The utilization of our imagination is an opportunity to step beyond the norms of our words, actions, and thoughts. It is astonishing. Everything that we can see or touch has stemmed from the imagination of a dreamer.

We have been provided with an ability to conceive ideas and then express them through the manifestation of our personal touch. From out of the darkness of a thought comes forth a seed for what may someday become reality. In times of exploration, there cannot be any limitations. Dream big and don't ever be ashamed of what others may say or think. It is the unfettered power of your thoughts, accompanied by a harmony of like-minded people who will help you create some of the most beautiful expressions the world has ever seen.

Honing your creativity requires being flexible in your thinking so that your ideas have an opportunity to transcend across an artistic horizon. Stop trying to view things from other's perspectives. Each of us is unique in our own way. Step outside of your comfort zone and try looking at things from a different angle. Perhaps what you envision may be the next big phenomenon.

Not everyone will be able to grasp the wonders of your creativity, but this is what separates you from the rest—your vision. Sit back, have a little fun with challenging yourself to come up with abnormal concepts. Maybe the composition of music awaits your gift. Regardless of what your calling in life may be, remember to imagine things in a creative way. Only those who dare to explore fruitful alternatives will be worthy of remembrance in history.

Jewel

> Dream, dream, dream, without feeling pressured to insert a comma, period, or any mark of conformity.
>
> —Jamar Jr.

Lesson 18:

The Burden of Excuses

> Ninety-nine percent of failures come from people who have a habit of making excuses.
>
> —George Washingtin Carver

Excuses are the cheapest commodities in the world. They are similar to opinions; everyone has one waiting to be thrust upon anyone willing to embrace them. No man or woman with a purpose should handicap their potential by making excuses. It is characteristic of lazy people to offer a poor explanation for why they failed to accomplish their goals for the day. Such people generally have a lot to say while their desire to succeed continues to linger, inactively. Before we can give sincere thought to being successful, first, we must honestly access the excuses we make for our failures:

- I didn't have a family who cared about me...
- I didn't finish school...
- I'm not smart enough...
- I don't have the time...
- If I wasn't in debt...
- I'm too tired...
- I don't know how to formulate a plan...
- I *wish* I could do certain things...
- I'm not good with accepting criticism...
- I'll get it done tomorrow...
- It's impossible to dream when you're stuck in the ghetto...
- My mind wanders all over the place...
- If my health was better...
- If I had better luck...
- If I didn't have a bad record...

And *blah, blah, blah!* Excuses have been around since the beginning of time. There is nothing wrong with you that a little self-discipline couldn't cure. Life is a game of chess and if you continue to come up with reasons for why you failed to make a plausible move, you will be checkmated every single time. Excuses are for weak-minded people.

The only thing preventing you from succeeding in life is *YOU!* It takes heart to get up every day and go make something out of nothing. Regardless of what your life may be like, no one is going to take care of you better than yourself.

> *Successful people have a low tolerance for those who continually create excuses.*
>
> —Tymir Johnson

Lesson 19:

Intelligence Cannot Be Seen Over the Backdrop of Stupidity

> *The ignorant praises his own ignorance.*
>
> **—African proverb**

There is no justification for failing to exercise good judgment unless it is your aim to be known as a fool. A thinker rarely stands accused of lacking common sense. When someone consistently remarks on the flaws of your character, it may be time to reevaluate yourself. I have a question: If we truly believe we're on top of our game, why do we continually find ourselves wallowing at the bottom?

Wise people move with a purpose. They seldom put themselves in a position to become the laughingstock of their peers. Look around you. Have you yet to realize there have been highly successful people who've ruined their careers and suffered insurmountable embarrassment because they made a poor decision? All it takes is a single moment of absentmindedness and everything you have worked so hard to achieve disappears. Once your character becomes tarnished, your honor will be destroyed forever.

The spotlight is now on you. It's show time! Spare yourself the humiliation of being harshly judged due to your actions and speech. Do you wish for your character to be exemplary or not? You may want to choose quickly before the world discovers who you really are. You possess invaluable jewels that will help you shine as bright as a beacon. Cast your light so the people can see what inspiration looks like. Make it commonplace to use your head for something other than a hat rack, for a wise person would never elect to dishonor their abilities. Through suffered ignorance and imprudent acts, character will ultimately meet its demise.

Jewel

> *You cannot be a clown and run the circus.*
>
> —Siani B.

Lesson 20:

The Nobility of a Promise

> *I have already agreed to be there and that is the same as if I gave you my head and my heart... I won't try to take back what I have said I will do as I told you I would.*
>
> **—Western Apache Tribal Member**

How can anyone have faith in you if you ignore the importance of honoring your word, your pledge, your oath, your vow, even your assurance to do as you have said? A promise is a commitment that shouldn't require witnesses to affirm your declarations. Integrity and love of self should be more than enough. Should you have no intent on doing what you say, why mislead others to believe otherwise? Your word is your bond!

There's no greater sorrow than an unfulfilled promise crushed by the weight of disappointment. You must never be selective when honoring your word. It is unfair to cherry-pick those worthy of a covenant while everyone else is subjected to being deceived. Your word is binding regardless of who you give it to. Once you have agreed to do something, failure to honor your promise will leave an unpleasant opinion of you in the minds of good people. Not only will you be seen as a fraud, but you'll also suffer from an imbalanced character. Before you give your word, *think*. Never hastily agree to things asked of you. Do not overcommit and, as a result, allow the pressure of more demanding obligations to cause you to falter on your promises.

Let there be distance between yourself and those unwilling to honor their word. They aren't good to themselves, and they won't be any good to you. Either you are striving to become a better person, or you are content with being as you are. It's your choice, but whichever it is, it will unquestionably highlight the strengths or defects of what you're made of. Through honoring your promises, your name will never cease to be remembered, even after you have long departed from this earth. It should be a pleasure to know that people smile when your name is mentioned.

A good name lives for eternity.

—Mia Terry-Johnson

Lesson 21:

The Sunset of Faith

> *Difficulties break some men but make others. No axe is sharp enough to cut the soul of a sinner who keeps on trying, one armed with hope that he will rise even in the end.*
>
> —Nelson Mandela

Hope: the fuel of our soul. It can empower us with motivational thoughts that may someday inspire the world; it is the summoning of ancestral strength and wisdom that lies dormant inside our DNA; it is confidence in a brighter, more meaningful tomorrow. Never permit it to escape your grasp. Let it shine with the belief that there is nothing more precious, because as long as you possess it, the womb of time will bear tasteful fruit.

What is a person without vision for the future? *Hopeless!* When we lose hope, our thoughts become fragmented, and we begin to act out of desperation without regard for the consequences. Embrace hope with an appreciation for its potential, because in doing so, you will never worry yourself with thoughts of being helpless. Faith will encourage you to strive for something greater than what you see. When being inspired by hope, don't waste it on daydreaming. Know within your heart that you can make all things come to fruition.

I am obligated to caution you against abusing the power of hope because solely relying upon it could hamper your ability to make meaningful progress. Having hope is a beautiful thing, but without physically applying yourself it will quickly lose its luster. God loves helping those of us who put forth an effort to help ourselves first. Logic is defied by the thought of expecting Him to do anything before we attempt to lift a finger. Never be so presumptuous.

> *Faith is the energy that we need to continue pressing on.*
>
> —**Anye Crawford**

Lesson 22:

The Crippling Effects of Running the Streets

> *When you stop chasing the wrong things, you give the right things a chance to catch up.*
>
> **—Anonymous**

I think it's time we have an honest conversation. For many of us, the streets are all that we've ever known. For a long time we have found comfort in them without the slightest curiosity for what tomorrow could look like if we applied ourselves. There are two sides to every coin. Perhaps this might be the perfect time to describe what awaits on the opposite side of fool's gold . . .

There seems to be an alarming number of us who glorify the stature of a gangster, but for some reason the repercussions of their actions go unheeded until after it has become too late. Let me guess, you thought you were untouchable and slicker than motor oil, too, huh? I don't mean to burst your bubble, but aspirations of being a gangster are overrated. Take a moment to reflect on what became of all the tough guys you knew of. Hurting people is wrong! It robs us of decency and taxes our soul.

Everything that we do wrong today will have serious consequences. Many of us will become mentally and emotionally sickened by burdens that will be impossible to hide from. When nights of restlessness arise, remember your atrocities from yesterday. Every insensible act that we commit against others must be paid for. Maybe it won't be today, but we certainly will pay. Would you care to know the disturbing aspects of it? It may be someone dear to you who will eventually pay the price for your actions.

There are many people who would like to know what our infatuation with guns is about. They aren't toys! They are dangerous weapons that have the potential to cause mass destruction and insurmountable grief. Do you not realize that an apology cannot adequately compensate for our reckless actions and lack of regard for the value of someone's life? Whether you accidentally or intentionally deprive a person of life, what could you possibly say to their family that could help relieve their pain? Absolutely nothing! A talented person has no business doing anything that would jeopardize their freedom, but a senseless person wouldn't think twice about what they stand to lose.

Remember the spiritual debt we owe? Don't worry about that yet, there will be a universal debt that must be collected first. In the meantime, prison *waits*. It's a harsh place where you will be denied the right to be human. Generosity will be substituted for barbarism. What does that mean? It means that before you can visit your family, correctional officers will require you to take off your clothes and assume a compromising position until they are satisfied that you are not concealing contraband in a place where the sun doesn't shine. The process will leave you feeling humiliated and embarrassed. The act itself will linger in your mind forever. But this is what you were in such a rush to experience, right? There will be no compassion, so do not look for any; if you enjoy loud and fruitless conversation that's exactly what you'll get. There will be practically no stimulating conversations to engage in. What verbal pleasure could one lost soul provide to another? There will be no unity. Everyone will be concerned with only themselves. You will be on your own, rotting away in a dark prison cell.

Wait! Stop the press. That reality is what you were expecting, right? All because you thought school wasn't for you. Sadly, you bet there would never be a need for reading, writing and math skills in your line of business. Instead of preparing for success, you chose to run the streets with those who were only *pretending* to be "about that life!" Because you have a bunch of fancy tattoos, you acted as if they would exempt you from thinking before you spoke. What a waste of precious brain cells.

The penitentiary is not a luxury club. It's a harsh place where your thoughts become warped, and your swag slowly fades away. Are you listening to what I am trying to tell you? *Prison* will be a lonely reality where you will be deprived of thinking for yourself. Very few people, outside of family, will be concerned with how you're doing, let alone what you need. Each day you will awaken to wishful thinking! What does that mean? It means, more than likely you are someone who's burnt their bridges and now that you're at the bottom, you've found yourself wishing you could undo your wrongs and erase your stupidity. Consequently, due to your reckless behavior, those who love you will believe it's better for you to be in prison than on the streets. As hurtful as it may be, from their point of view, at least now they won't have to worry about being awakened by a disturbing knock on the door, heralding unfortunate news of you being shot dead. *I tried warning you.*

There are people older than us for a reason. None of them are as stupid as you think. They have been around the block a lot more than we have. Respect should always be given to those who care enough to be on your case about doing the right things. From our perspective it may seem as though they are nagging us for no reason. But these are the same people who would do anything within their power to help us, and this is the thanks they get? There aren't too many people who will love us the way they do. Besides, if they are as horrible as you say, then why are they the first persons you call when you need help? You see it's like this—if you didn't act irresponsible no one would be on your back about the small things. Use your head.

Strive to make your family proud instead of ashamed to reveal their biological relationship to you. We only get so many bites at the apple before our credibility becomes mush. Once that occurs, it will take a long time to demonstrate that we have changed enough to warrant giving us another shot at the title. When your actions resemble that of a fool, providing additional chances becomes too risky. No one wants to be criticized for going out on a limb for someone who was never deserving of it. Think before you act or speak impulsively. An undisciplined mind will sooner or later create huge problems. Slow down! Follow the signs that are all around you. It is better to be slow and steady than to become a statistic due to your unwillingness to follow basic instructions.

    The truth is, your so-called friends who do a sloppy job pretending that they care only want to use you. In their world, it's better for you to get into trouble than them. When you follow behind people and act like you can't think for yourself, you will end up paying a costly price. When you're sitting in prison, your buddies will never make the time to see if you're okay mentally, physically, or financially. Nor will they check on your family. Would you like to know what they will do? They'll talk about how dumb you are.

    Don't be in such a hurry to punish yourself. When the curtains have been tugged open and you realize that you're locked in a cage, it's extremely hard to find things worth smiling about. The jokes will be at

The Crippling Effects of Running the Streets

your expense and if you are a realist you will have to admit that every day you feel like a fool. As a constant reminder of your stupidity, all you'll have to do is look at the jester's costume the prison issued you.

The moral of the story is: No one is ready to attend your funeral because you chose to be hardheaded and run the streets with the wrong crowd. Your mother, father, aunt, nor grandparents are prepared to lose you. Stop acting like carrying guns and selling drugs is a way to validate your masculinity. It won't! It will only reveal your lack of intelligence.

In prison there are a lot of grown men who cry at night due to the pain of their actions. All the prayers in the world won't bring someone back after you have deprived them of living. Behind those steel bars and concrete walls, you will be forced to deal with the consequences of your poor decisions for the rest of your natural born life. There is no hiding from your demons. Either you're a good person or you have a wicked spirit that needs to be contained. How you choose to walk your path of life will speak volumes about who you truly are. Look around, your days are too precious to be wasted on tears filled with sorrow.

Certain violations may never be forgiven regardless of how sincere the apology is.

—Jason A. Crawford

Lesson 23:

Much Is Missed When You Are Talkative

> *Wise men talk because they have something to say; fools because they have to say something.*
>
> —**Plato**

Why do we have such an insatiable desire to be chatterboxes? Perhaps it wouldn't be so troublesome if we were offering something of value; something that would be more comforting than recycled rumors; something that would contribute to another person's journey; or that would exhibit the depth of our intelligence rather than highlight a lack of courtesy. There are no benefits to being talkative. Are you an educator or a motivational speaker? Then why must you seize every chance you see to inject your opinion? In the precious moments that we spend being longwinded, an opportunity to appreciate what the next person is trying to say is lost.

Talking solely for the sake of hearing ourselves speak is not only a waste of valuable energy, but also a selfish display of our manners. Proverbs 21:23 of the Bible says, "He who guards his mouth and his tongue keeps himself from calamity." The Holy Qur'an, in Sura 3, Iyat 19 mentions, "And be moderate in your talking, and lower your voice. Verily, the harshest of all voices is the braying of asses."

Far too many of us are of the opinion that we must always have the last word in a squabble. What a flawed characteristic to possess. Those who insist on being argumentative do not realize that there is strength in saying nothing at all. The last word doesn't need to be verbalized. Why is that? It's because a thinker understands exactly what's being conveyed through abstaining from speaking. Silence implies that you are disciplined and that perhaps your best response is taking place in the depths of your mind.

Beware of those who do nothing but talk, talk, talk. All their blathering will tell you not only who they are, but how thoughtless. Why should someone with such a character defect be worthy of an occasion to align themselves with you? A distinguished individual will do their absolute best to refrain from speaking more than they should. Too much talking exposes the secrets of a good thing, in which case it becomes no good for anyone. Silence provides your character with mysteriousness. Always leave something for the curiosity of others' imaginations.

Jewel

> Control your impulse to speak more than you have to.
>
> **—James Ballard**

Lesson 24:

Desire Earnestly

> To desire is to yearn for success.
>
> —Timothy Butler

Our psyche is more powerful than we are aware of. Aside from those who know the secrets to obtaining success, very few people pay attention to the importance of cultivating desire and an aptitude for thinking creatively. If you cannot visualize your goals, they will not be given a chance to transform into something substantive. You must have a burning desire for whatever it is that you want from life. Time will not wait, and neither will the intangible forces of the universe.

When you have decided that you want something

bad enough, that moment must be met with determination and perseverance. Let nothing nor anyone deter you from fulfilling an urgency to pursue your heart's desire. Many people have made the mistake of dismissing an idea as unrealistic or improbable before thoroughly exploring its feasibility. It may be that single idea that will thrust you amongst some of the world's greatest inventors. A desire to achieve what you want from life, regardless of what it is, must be met with the same zeal that you have to survive from day-to-day. Every successful person can attest to the power of desire. It is what has fueled their dreams.

> *There is no royal flower-strewn path to success. And if there is I have not found it, for if I have accomplished anything in life it is because I have been willing to work hard.*
>
> **—Madame C.J. Walker**

Through the perfection of Madame Walker's vision, the world shall never forget her many contributions. Not everyone who is famous has been acquainted with education or the comforts of wealth while pursuing their ambitions. Madame C.J. Walker was born to parents who were slaves, and yet, despite her personal conflicts she triumphed, becoming the first African-American self-made millionaire. Ms. Walker's desire was to create hair products that could remedy women's hair loss. Ingeniously, she went on to invent hair care products and a host of cosmetics.

Likewise, Henry Ford had minimal exposure to a formal education. He didn't profess to know everything, but he was smart enough to know exactly who to call to get the job done correctly. Unfortunately, after carefully selecting a team of capable engineers, they soon became convinced that it was impossible to create an eight-cylinder engine. Determined to transcend the unconceivable, Mr. Ford continued to press them for results. Through persistence and his vision for what could be, the engineers eventually accomplished their goal. *Anything in life is possible if you are determined to win.*

A wise old man once said, "Sometimes you will have to go where you don't want to be in order to learn the things you need to know." The genius that is entwined in our DNA must be provided with a chance to fully evolve. Solitude has a way of enriching our ideas; fertilizing the seeds of our wildest imaginations;

and expounding on their usefulness through days, months, and sometimes years of perfection.

You shouldn't expect to reap what you desire until you are ready in mind and heart. Have faith in your abilities. If there is something you don't know, do not be afraid to ask someone who may be able to help. All desires originate in our subconscious. If you would like to make your sense of desire stronger, each night before you go to bed, write down a list of your goals and read them aloud at least three times. It is a well-known fact that reading before we go to sleep helps our minds better retain what we've read. Speak what you want into existence. Acquaint yourself with the power of desire and the forces of nature will happily reward your efforts someday.

If the intensity of your desire is strong enough, there will exist no hurdle that can hinder you from grasping success.

Lesson 25:

Perseverance Strengthens Your Character

> There are a number of ethnic people who've had to horrifically endure and continue persevering in the name of making sure that their story was adequately preserved.
>
> —Quamir Johnson

Regardless of what your life consists of, you owe it to yourself to persevere until the storm has passed. You are a fighter. It's in your nature to demonstrate you can endure and overcome what is seemingly insurmountable. Whenever you set out to accomplish a goal, do not worry about how long it will take before things materialize. Set your eyes on the prize and remain steadfast. Each step should provide you with a refreshing view of your objective. Stay the course and you will find inspiration in places you least expect.

Perseverance and persistence are relatives, as each of them encourage you to continue fighting, resisting, and striving to conquer the notion of being easily defeated. What place you finish in a marathon means very little; honor is bestowed upon those who find the courage to complete the race; slow and steady, as opposed to impatient and reckless, wins the race. If you truly understand what it means to persevere then you can certainly speak about the light at the end of the tunnel. When you emerge, regardless of how battered you may be, admiration from the well-wishers will be there to embrace you. Be sure to compliment your character for the strength that it took to endure and get things done. You really should be proud of yourself. The world is full of people who refuse to put forth effort to improve their circumstances.

Sometimes the cards we are dealt look as if they've been stacked. Sorry, but you, too, must be tested just as everyone who came before you. When difficult times arise, find the serenity to allow your personal wisdom to guide you. It will never lead you astray.

Neither family nor friends will always grasp your vision. This is when you will prove to be your most valued ally. There will be journeys that you will have to undertake alone, solely because others won't have your drive or best interest at heart. Not everyone will relate to your passion, your ideas, or your desire to do something that requires stepping outside of the box. Don't spend too much time trying to figure them out. Persevere with faith in what you are doing. When you least expect it, your hard work and ability to keep on keeping on will reveal what you are genuinely made of.

> *Some of life's most rewarding perks go to those who refuse to quit.*
>
> **—Siani B.**

Lesson 26:

The Seeds of Our Circumstances

> *If you are displeased with your conditions, sit quietly, reflect a bit, then supplement your ambitious thoughts with a heap of action.*
>
> **—James E. Ballard**

Suppose you were the subject of a spirited conversation, and someone remarked, "You are the captain of your ship, master gardener of your soul, and influencer of current and future circumstances." Would you agree or would you think that person had a screw loose? Before you answer, let's take a mental spin. I would like you to carefully look around your environment. What do you see—

impoverishment, a story of success, complacency, or maybe a love for ease? If you will allow me, I would like to share a few precious jewels with you:

- Just as cultivated or uncultivated gardens bear fruit of their kind, so, too, shall the seeds of our thoughts spring forth. Meaning, if your thought-pattern consists of self-crippling images, your circumstances will reflect such. However, should your thoughts represent ambitious ideas capable of guiding you towards realizing your destiny, in time your conditions will transform.

- We must stop living life as if we are victims of our circumstances, because even if it were so, such useless crutches should never suffice for our reluctance to maneuver around the limitations that are self-imposed. If in your mind and heart you believe you can accomplish anything, you will. But should you contemplate discord, even for a second, your failure will become inevitable.

- It is time to permit our imaginations to soar. Many of us are the authors of resilient stories;

pilots of jumbo jets; and architects of ingenious mansions. We are where we are so that we may learn how to get to where we are supposed to be. Only creative thinkers advance in life. The world stands ready to assist anyone who can demonstrate a willingness to step outside of their comfort zone to zealously pursue ideas. Get up, get out there and get you some. Life and all of its glories have been waiting for a long time to see how we will reclaim our rightful positions among those who are ambitious by nature.

- There is an old saying, "The mind is a terrible thing to waste." Before we can make progress, we must first tune-up our ability to *think deeply*; the smooth talker dressed in fancy clothes may be a shammer. Too often acts of greed, impatience, or desperation sway us to focus on the dangling carrot as opposed to analyzing the intentions of the person dangling it. *For every cause there is an effect!* As you create mentally, persistence, faith in self, and hard work will eventually provide you with a prosperous harvest.

- God has blessed us with the faculty to think big, dream endlessly and imagine what could someday be, but it comes with a price that requires us to seriously ponder things beyond physical appearances. A wise woman once said, "Mankind shrinks from no task more swiftly than thinking for self. For it is considered by many to be laborious and unnecessary." No wonder we continuously find ourselves unhappy. Depending on where you are positioned, it appears as though we have given up and permitted others to make crucial decisions for us.

If you are serious about changing your conditions, use your mind wisely and align yourself with those who understand the value in being a sower! Rearrange your thoughts. In time your circumstances will dutifully alter themselves.

The Seeds of Our Circumstances

Discomfort and mental agitation
may be a sign that it is time to
move in a new direction.

Lesson 27:

The Benefits of Punctuality

> One's ability to be punctual is indicative of a commitment to redeem time.
>
> —Karen Bombgarner

If there is a lack of interest for being on time, how will we prosper? Punctuality isn't selective, it is a courtesy that should be extended to everyone, regardless of social status. Unfortunately, some people believe that being observant of an appointment is overrated. No wonder the early bird has lost its knack for catching the morning worm. Possessing the ability to be on time for school, commitments, or family gatherings speaks to who you are and whether you are responsible.

Unquestionably, things will occur which can cause

us to be late. Should this become your reality, act responsibly by calling or sending a text stating you're running behind time. There is no need for excuses such as, "I overslept" or "something came up at the last minute" or "I was unable to find a babysitter in time." Any attempt to justify your reasoning for your tardiness will only make matters worse.

Being prompt unveils a picture of someone who has respect for others. As a result, it instills confidence in those who may be considering you for a better position. If you tell someone that you will be somewhere at a specified time, be a steward of your word. It is highly important that we remain mindful of our commitments. Those who have a few things on the ball will be reluctant to embrace anyone who has a history of being late.

The hours of a day are more than numbers chronologically arranged on the face of a clock.

Lesson 28:

Patience Can Enhance the Fortitude of Your Character

> *You must eat the elephant one bite at a time.*
>
> **—Twi proverb**

For many people, life has been full of hardships. And even if it were not, for those who possess the strength to appropriately manage pain, misfortunes, or provocation without complaint or allowing their anger to spill over, it would still serve as a remarkable show of patience. Not everyone can remain calm while exploring different options. Some folks will become antsy due to delays, others will jump the gun out of frustration with little regard for what could have been had they shown forbearance. Self-control is a component of patience. It signifies one's ability to critically think as things naturally progress. How is a tree to someday provide the cover of shade if there is no tolerance for the development of its leaves? Who will task us with leading others if we are unable to recognize the value of favorable positioning?

One of America's most prestigious museums, dedicated to the heroic men and women of September 11, 2001, took years of patiently planning before being unveiled for the world to see. Question: Who are we that we know not a semblance of patience? Anything that has potential for growth must do so at its appointed time. Likewise, you, too, must learn how to wait before witnessing your moment come to light.

Oftentimes out of habit, we provide shelter to intolerance. As a result, we become acquainted with discontent, selfishness, and irritability. By developing patience, it allows the small things to remain what they are—unimportant. The last thing you ever want to do is provide someone with an opportunity to see your character lacking during trying times. It's about perfecting your mental discipline. When the impulse of intolerance appears, try to turn down the volume. Find the fortitude to remain focused on the bigger picture.

Always pay attention to your inner voice. It knows exactly what you need and when. Just sit quietly, listen, and have confidence that you will ultimately prevail. You may actually be able to see what materializes after you have learned to perfect the art of waiting patiently.

Jewel

Patience is the essence of a flower's existence.

Lesson 29:

The Story of Lazybones

> *There are two cardinal sins from which all others spring; impatience and laziness.*
>
> **—Franz Kafka**

If we expect to find our place amongst God's creations, we'll have to put forth our best effort without cutting corners—responsibilities must be fulfilled, school assignments need to be completed, relationships have to be honored, and every task placed before us will have to be carried out to the best of our abilities. And that, my friend, is simply a starting point. Before progress appears you will have to demonstrate a willingness to consistently apply yourself in everything that you partake in.

Never let it be said that you were someone who had a habit of doing things halfheartedly, nor were you someone whose tasks, chores, or assignments were completed slothfully. Nothing about a slacker is cool. In fact, it can prevent you from discovering your true potential. You are no longer a child. That was a moment in the stream of life when you were validly entitled to handouts. Today is a new day, one which requires every person to prove they can hold their own.

Remember this: very little comes to a clock-watcher except for wishful thoughts. Regardless of what you want in life, whether it's a nice house, lots of money, or a better education, you must work hard for it. The potential for greatness is in all of us, but if we fail to develop the faculties which will best suit our aspirations, we stand a strong chance of losing the game. Your spirit isn't broken, so why are you waiting for others to do for you before attempting to do for yourself? Ambition is what will propel you above mediocrity. This is the perfect time to get out there and make something happen. When embarking upon any task, complete it as if it was the best thing that ever happened for you.

Life is active, not passive. When you spot a man or woman unwilling to do for themselves, you have found a person who doesn't mind basking in lazy mental habits. Stay far away from them. Their do-nothing nature can be highly contagious. If you have any intentions of developing a strong character, you must surround yourself with like-minded people. Every day should be utilized, trying to make your dreams come true. Very few things will come easy until we have learned the value of working for what we want.

Jewel

> Sadly, lazy people rarely find anything wrong with scraps, while those who aspire for greatness partake in the benefits of a full course meal.

Lesson 30:

The Importance of Good Listening

> *When you talk, you are only repeating what you already know. But if you listen you may learn something new.*
>
> —Dalai Lama

If I inconsiderately speak while you are speaking, then how can we effectively communicate? Being a good listener takes patience and a genuine interest in understanding what others are trying to say. That entails paying attention to the person talking, waiting for a natural pause before responding, and, when appropriate, making eye contact.

The Importance of Good Listening

Often we tend to cause people to feel as if what they have to say is unimportant. Why? Some of us have become used to injecting our opinion before honoring the balance (speaking and listening) of a conversation. Have you ever given a thought to why God has provided us with two ears and one mouth? He intended for us to listen twice as much as we are to speak. When others are expressing themselves, our silence can be very powerful. It not only demonstrates respect for them, but it also proves that your time is no more important than what they have to say. Every conversation deserves a breather to wisely reflect on what was said.

Ask yourself, "Have I carefully listened before impatiently chiming in?" If you answered "no," more than likely you may have missed an opportunity to build upon the foundation of a promising relationship. You see, we listen to understand other people's choices. We listen to empathize. We listen to find appreciation. We listen to be supportive. We listen to identify those who must be avoided. We listen to discover those who consistently speak in excess. We listen to absorb the wisdom of those who know more than us.

Attentively listening is a skill that takes discipline and practice before perfecting. Everyone has a right to be heard without being interrupted by unguarded commentary. Forgive me, but every time someone speaks, it does not qualify us to offer an opinion. The world is bigger than you and I, so it's essential for us to prove that we are capable of graciously conducting ourselves at all times.

Jewel

> Courage is what it takes to stand up and speak; courage is also what it takes to sit down and listen.
>
> **—Winston Churchill**

Lesson 31:

A Quitter Could Never Become King or Queen

> *Even in your moments of exhaustion, you must keep both eyes on the person who has a habit of running from difficulties.*
>
> —Joanne Brown

Go ahead. Take some time to reflect on the struggles and challenges of your journey. This would be the perfect day to commend yourself for not allowing life to beat you down. Your persistence, fueled by visions of obtaining something better than what you currently have, has inspired you to keep pressing on. And for that reason alone, there can be no greater compliment than being recognized for the strength of your mind! Unfortunately, not everyone has your fortitude, so a cautionary heads up is warranted: Under no circumstances should you entertain thoughts of giving up before it is time.

One of the biggest mistakes we make is throwing in the towel when a situation becomes difficult to manage, or when adversity winks at our intelligence, or when the naysayers emerge with a barrage of criticisms. Stay focused! This is the hour you have been waiting for to christen your ship, *captain*. Surely you're not considering turning back, are you? If so, maybe it's time to reexamine your priorities. You see, after the skipper has set out to sea and comes across a storm brewing on the horizon, he/she doesn't have the luxury of thinking about their best interest. Duty has charged them with the responsibility of making sure everyone aboard safely arrives at their destinations.

Hasn't anyone explained to you that before experiencing a major accomplishment, it is probable that you will encounter a brief stint of failure? But that shouldn't give you a reason to give up and move on to something new. Maybe a perfect time to change your perspective is when things become challenging. After all, a problem is nothing more than a scrambled puzzle waiting for someone to logically piece it together. Try developing a habit of looking beyond obvious roadblocks in expectation of bumping into classic realities. This thing we call *life* is serious business. You, too, will be shaken up, scrambled, and tested before a determination is made as to whether your daily efforts qualify for a stamp of authenticity.

Each day God grants us permission to awaken, we must go out into the world with an eagerness to do our best. Do not be afraid to fully apply yourself. In the heart of a stranger, who's been watching you toll without complaints, may lie an opportunity that has your name written on it. Keep that in mind the next time you consider being a quitter. If you truly intend to secure a place among those who are worthy of remembrance, you will have to prove that you possess "stick-to-itiveness."

> *Never accept anything from someone who runs from the sight of their own shadow.*
>
> —Anthony Sharp

Lesson 32:

The Harmony of Unity

> *When spider webs unite, they can tie up a lion.*
>
> **—African proverb**

If two carpenters were tasked with building a deck, four additional hands would be helpful, but six or nine would accomplish the goal more swiftly. There is and will forever be incontestable strength in numbers. Together we prevail, but divided we will continuously suffer defeat. So, where do we go from here, you ask? Perhaps *we* could begin by asking, "At what point in life did it become okay for us to only think of ourselves?"

The Harmony of Unity

> *I believe in the brotherhood of men, all men, but I don't believe in brotherhood with anybody who doesn't want brotherhood with me. I believe in treating people right, but I'm not going to waste my time trying to treat somebody right who doesn't know how to return the treatment.*
>
> —Malcolm X

Ahhh. The sentiment of your brother, treating you as he would want to be treated, and your sister likewise. You shouldn't expect people to stand in solidarity with you, unless you are willing to do the same for them. Unity is the synchronization of multiple voices harmoniously resounding as one; it is the masses willing to sacrifice and work towards common interests, together.

Unquestionably, unity demands that you stand with us, and we stand with you. Welcome. You have just been introduced to a concept more favorable than a boastful love for self! Only through establishing reciprocal alliances can we effectively combat injustice. The way I see it, liberty is a precious gift from the Creator of the Universe. Who are we to act so dispassionate when robbing people of their self-worth?

Our ranks will never entirely be depleted of traitors. When you do find them, quickly escort them to the nearest exit. Their only aim is to sow havoc and confusion. Unfortunately, some people were meant to be nothing more than who they are. Rarely, if ever, will they see anything wrong with violating boundaries and you mustn't waste your time trying to get them to understand their infractions.

To find mentally and spiritually strong people unified for a common purpose is a rarity. Why? Most of us act as if it's blasé to extend trust when a need arises for us to come together for anything worth fighting for. Look in the mirror. Can you see it? Once the passion of a brave spirit has been provoked, there shouldn't be anything that we cannot accomplish together. Standing unified must be a collective effort where everyone feels a duty to contribute. One person could never be the life force of a coalition, no more than a single thread can make up a spider's web. True unity is without selfish, fragmented components.

> When a vision filled with inspiration emerges, nothing less than a unified effort will bring it to fruition.
>
> —Tim Butler

Lesson 33:

Good People Never Forget Kind Acts

> When you are kind to someone in trouble, you hope they'll remember and be kind to someone else, and it'll become like wildfire.
>
> **—Whoopi Goldberg**

If I act neighborly to you, it's only right that you act neighborly to me. For through such mutuality, we can discover the good embedded in each other's heart. Consider for a moment: How would you feel if you were constantly surrounded by people who were inconsiderate, or too much to bear? Now imagine what the world might be like without the touch of selfless people. It wouldn't be so welcoming, would it?

There is no reason for any of us to go around acting rude or stingy towards each other. Being kind doesn't cost you anything; in fact, if you act from the depths of your heart, you might attract a blessing or two. Each day provides us with more than enough time to exemplify the generosity of our character, and tenderness of our favor. Responding to someone's need for assistance is an act of kindness; offering leniency to those who have proven to be worthy illustrates kindness; and financially helping an elderly person who may not be able to pay a bill, shows the compassion of a kind heart.

Your inclination to give must never be expressed in hopes of receiving recognition for the good that you've done. When you do for others, be certain that your actions are executed because it's what makes you feel good inside. Either goodwill is forged in your soul or it's not. Not everyone has it in them to ask, "Is there something I can do for you?" or "May I help carry your groceries to your car?" Sometimes a simple hug speaks volumes.

Despite your temporary woes, people have a right to know who you are, what cloth you're cut from and what type of substance is behind your words. An elderly man once said, "When someone reveals the contents of their heart, don't make the mistake of thinking they are anything other than what they have shown you!" A person can only pretend for so long. Sooner or later, they will slip up and reveal their true nature.

You must protect your kindness. It is quickly fading from our way of life. You should be kind to everyone, but when unconditionally giving of yourself, it should be well guarded.

Jewel

> *Some people are naturally filled with kind words and sympathy; others will only reveal such characteristics on certain occasions.*

Lesson 34:

Do Not Allow Anger to Rouse You

> *People who fly into a rage always make a bad landing.*
>
> **—Will Rogers**

Take a deep breath. That's it, try to relax before you unintentionally say or do something you'll later regret. If you muster up the strength to do that, it will demonstrate an ability to control your feelings. But if you cannot, it means that you will need to work on your proactive solutions.

Anger can be a dangerous emotion. It can cause us to take things personally, cloud our judgment, overlook plausible solutions, and react under false pretense. Once provoked, it fuels irrational thoughts and behaviors, making it virtually impossible to maturely address the problem. We all can relate to what it's like to be agitated, ticked off, or see red, but how many of us know how to intelligently navigate stormy emotions?

Accepting responsibility for our behavior is golden; however, accepting responsibility for our emotions is extraordinary. In life things won't always be to our liking. Unfortunately, people will intentionally misstate their gripe, be overly critical of you and misspeak without consideration of your feelings, but that should never prevent you from reacting constructively. Your thoughts, your emotions, and your comments and behavior all belong to you. No one can make you do anything you don't want to do. When angered, if you choose to react emotionally, it's on you! On the flip side of the coin, should you elect to be a thinker who resolves conflicts before things erupt, you will be credited for being emotionally strong-minded.

Here's the thing—very few of us have been taught the value of thinking before we lose control. If we are unable to pause in the moments before feeling emotionally triggered, how will we be able to consider the situation objectively?

Do Not Allow Anger to Rouse You

In the midst of being angry, if you can at least make sense of what has gotten you to your boiling point, that is more than enough time to think twice. Good habits create positive outcomes. Every emotionally charged response should be countered by exhaling, self-talk, a countdown from a fixed number, or walking away. Thinking before you react is an excellent way to sharpen your social skills. It is extremely difficult to undo the damage we cause while in the wake of our personal madness.

When something is bothering you, speak on it. Confide in someone you trust. Journal, exercise or listen to your favorite music. Do anything, as long as it is constructive. Never walk around harboring feelings that may cause you to explode.

> *To spend a night in anger is better than to spend it in repentance."*
>
> **—Senegalese proverb**

The next time you become angry, try thinking about something you enjoyed doing or what you stand to lose. In that moment of joy, maybe you did something silly, and it warranted a laugh. It doesn't matter what type of thoughts they are, just as long as they're positive. Force a smile on your face and remember, a smile is worth more than the agony of realizing you don't always get a second chance.

Jewel

> *If you are patient in one moment of anger, you will escape a hundred days of sorrow.*
>
> **—Chinese proverb**

Lesson 35:

The Grace of a Tranquil Mind

> *An average loquacious person is someone to flee from.*
>
> **—Yoruba proverb**

Traveling the road of self-discovery is no easy task. It takes patience and courage to face our imperfections, and a willingness to be still long enough to appreciate the tranquility of our mind, body, and soul. Sit down for a moment. Take a few deep breaths, close your eyes and relax. Now, aside from the sound of worldly chaos, influential noise, or boisterous gossiping, what is it that you hear? Is it your inner voice, God's wisdom, or perhaps the pulsation of your heart? If it is not, it may be time to fine-tune the hub of your soul.

Regardless of where we go in life, every step should be taken under the guidance of disciplined emotions and a peaceful mind. In other words, through faithfully adhering to daily prayer, meditation, or time alone, we can restore the unbalanced parts of ourselves.

Internal silence isn't only essential to becoming a great thinker, it's also therapeutic. It can help clarify our perspective (differentiating between what we assume to be real versus what is), give birth to inspirational ideas, heal us psychologically, and call attention to our true calling. There are very few things more soothing than having an illuminated spirit and enlightened mind.

During the time of Jesus Christ, those who desired to perfect themselves did so by seeking refuge within caves, mountains, and monasteries. It's true. People would seclude themselves from all potential distractions in order to learn not only who they were, but what they were capable of becoming. It's important to find peace of mind when we can. Such valuable moments must be utilized to listen to our thoughts, evaluate our feelings, gather strength, and resist agitations. Absent a quiet mind, it is difficult to see our potential or grasp God's instructions. How can we grow if we are unable to hear our inner voice?

In quieting the commotion from within, it is also

important to abstain from speaking much. We must learn to reserve our comments. Look at well-composed men and women of the world. They, too, have their share of personal struggles, but there is something extremely alluring about their silence and tendency to speak only when it is absolutely necessary. Every word that comes to mind doesn't need to be verbalized. Listen to what's being said, analyze it and resist the urge to dignify speech that has no relevance. This is the power of a tranquil mind.

Jewel

> Ho who can master their inner silence can never be tricked by the semantics of a fast talker.

Lesson 36:

The Civility of Being Tactical

> *There is something impressive about a person who can defuse tensions diplomatically.*
>
> —Re'Nee Taylor

Never feel as though you must apologize for being who you are, or for the way people favorably respond to you. God gave all of us unique talents for a reason. All we have to do is learn to perfect them in a way that can help the next person move along. When shining your light upon the world, not everyone will approve of your charming personality, nor will they be inclined to follow your example. Some folks will despise you for no apparent reason, some will be jealous, and others will doubt you regardless of what you say. In such cases you will have to be tactful to get things done.

Sometimes the bridge of courtesy will be obstructed by people who have large egos, a lack of enthusiasm, an inability to work with others, a negative personality, or a knack for being disruptive. Therefore, a measured yet cordial response is essential. Keep in mind that a genuine concern for how someone is doing is a powerful icebreaker. It's okay to inquire about their day, how they're feeling, or just opening the door to provide them with an opportunity to be heard. Allow the warmth of your heart to lead the way when searching for words that can help you effectively communicate with those who act like a disastrous storm. Trying to argue with someone who is respectfully soothing is hard to do.

Being tactful is about utilizing diplomacy to resolve issues. It has been said, "You can catch more bees with honey than with vinegar." Never pass up an opportunity to be the person who elects to be well-mannered while in the midst of ignorance. Keep in mind: kindness is often an appropriate choice for a tasteless disposition.

It's not about what you say to people, it's how you articulate what you have to say to them.

—Allen Myers

Lesson 37:

Show Them You Are Cultured

> *The best effect of fine persons is felt after we have left their presence.*
>
> —Ralph Waldo Emerson

Ah, the pleasantness of a polished character that has acquired a taste for the finer things in life. The key to mental sophistication entails learning how to appreciate life's valued adventures. There are no established customs that state you must be fond of recitals or symphony concerts, but you should at least try to visit museums, music festivals, or Broadway plays in an attempt to enhance your cultural insights. Broaden your horizons. You might be surprised at how much you actually enjoy it. Since we have gained a new way of viewing the world, it's essential to expose ourselves to events that offer mental stimulation. Instead of going to the movies, attend a play, a cabaret, or book fair.

Having class doesn't mean you're conceited. It simply tells a story of you having matured and been exposed to qualitative events that are outside of the popular mainstream. Gentlewomen, being cultured signifies that someday you might choose the companionship of a mate who is capable of thinking and making his own way in life. Gentlemen, a showing of good taste will convey your resolve to gravitate to respectable women who have ambitions of forging their own path. An accumulation of mental jewels should be helpful in assisting with a touch of smoothness. The things you find delightful don't have to be expensive. They only need to expose you to tasteful events.

Remember: whenever you meet success and have the pleasure of mingling with people from different social statuses, it's important that you be cultured in some fashion. People who possess class rarely associate with those who are wretched and constantly in search of ways to get over.

When you know who you are, delight can be found in any conversation that pertains to something substantive.

Lesson 38:

The Art of a Good Conversation

> To win the hearts of others and always be welcomed, we must be cautious of our tone of voice and facial expression.
>
> —Shih Cheng Yen

You can possess admirable wisdom and recite the most eloquent fables, but it will count for very little if you cannot articulate your thoughts respectfully. A person who claims intelligence is soon discovered within the first words that come off their tongue. After the initial salutation, those who are without the ability to hold a constructive dialogue find themselves at a loss for words of expression. Good conversation is an art that requires a reservoir of tasteful vocabulary; nothing intimidating or fancy. It is thoughtfully crafted words with a hint of charm that will leave a lasting impression upon others. Whether you are interviewing for a job, engaged in small talk, or attempting to ask the love of your life for their hand in marriage, knowing how to communicate with a touch of class is important. How can we effectively network if we lack the ability to verbalize our ideas or needs?

There is never a shortage of substantive information when you engage in conversations with people who know a few things. Listen before speaking in hopes that you may grasp what you verbally receive from others. Do not be afraid to ask thoughtful questions that can present you with an opportunity to learn more about the person you are speaking with. If you approach every fruitful conversation with such delicateness, your discussions will never go unadorned.

Perhaps you can recall a time when you weren't doing so well emotionally and an inspirational conversation from a special person was able to lift your spirits. That is the essence of cultivating relationships through tasteful words, something a text message could never provide you with. Never lose your knack for mingling with the pleasures of a verbal exchange.

When conversing with others, know when to take a hint. Sometimes we tend to become long-winded without considering the value of others' time, or what they might be going through at the moment. Try to pay attention to the subtle signs: glancing at their watch, indiscriminate yawns, loss of eye contact, or an abrupt change in conversation. They're all indications that you may be speaking too much. Say what it is you have to say in as little time as possible.

Jewel

> *If your conversation has the effect of a good message, you will unquestionably receive immediate confirmation.*

Lesson 39:

The Importance of Values

> *Every time a value is born, existence takes on a new meaning; every time one dies, some part of that meaning passes away.*
>
> —Joseph W. Krutch

Values are the true wealth of our character. The foundation we vigilantly stand upon with a touch of defensiveness towards all violators. They are the standards and principles that make up an essential part of our lives. They are the compilation of everything that is important, and they govern our actions until our very last breath. No one can tell you what your values consist of. Each of us must take a deep look within to make such a discovery for ourselves.

For many, values consist of acting with integrity and being brutally honest with ourselves before attempting to be honest with others. It can be an uncompromising loyalty to your beliefs, exhibiting decency, or abiding by the rules even when you don't agree with the fairness of them. Rules are rules! Also, values may consist of prioritizing family before everyone else, being dutiful to your Lord, providing food to those who are less fortunate, being self-sufficient, or being unwilling to compromise the morals which they live by.

Values are what righteously guide us through our journey in life. They are what make us unique. You see, what may be of value to you, may be completely irrelevant to someone else. Once you learn what's important to you, do not go against it for any reason. Discover what your values are and never allow anyone to discourage you from honoring them.

The Importance of Values

Jewel

> *Values are what highlights the silent angels in all of us.*

Lesson 40:

The Imagination of a Visionary

> *A visionary is someone who envisions ideas that may potentially help make the world a better place to live.*
>
> —Paula Riddick

As a visionary in the midst of daydreaming, there will unceasingly be ignorant people who will attempt to discourage you by voicing their irritation with your dreaming. Ignore them! There is nothing wrong with being creative, a pioneer, or an innovator. A visionary foresees the potential of things. Question: While in the comforts of your imagination, how much do your ideas inspire you?

The Imagination of a Visionary

Allow me to tell you a few things about a visionary. We are dreamers of dreams. We are continuously in search of views, concepts, and schemes, irrespective of how unreasonable they may appear to be. A visionary understands the correlation between what our mind attracts in likeness and the significance of entertaining thoughts on a grand scale, something average folks usually claim to be a waste of time and uninteresting. But it's not. If you think about it, it's actually pretty amazing.

Oftentimes we stifle our creativity due to failing to pursue ideas with a curiosity for what could be. Many of us have great potential. We imagine things that seem to be laughable to others. Instead of seeking ways to express our concepts, we become intimidated and give up. Everything happens for a reason, just as for every cause, there is an effect. Don't ever stop utilizing your imagination. Enlarge your thoughts. Average minds will not be able to perceive the beauty of your visions. A castle builder will never limit their conscious abilities. There are very few people who can acknowledge their talent and gaze into tomorrow with intentions on exhibiting their best! A creative artist can sit somewhere quietly and escape to a realm that encourages their thoughts to grow and grow and grow until they become manifested.

After making appropriate revisions to your ideas, become a visionary who aspires to flourish. Your imagination has an invisible supply of intellectual talents that must be shared with the world. Although there will be people who lack your enthusiasm or act indifferent towards you, never allow anyone to persuade you to abandon your creativity. Should they burst out laughing at your ideas, smile with determination to prevail. Show others the value of grasping an elusive dream that just may endure the test of time. Remember, you don't have to know a visionary. If you are creative, you were born to be one.

If you don't build your dream, someone will hire you to help them build theirs.

—Dhirubhai Ambani

Lesson 41:

The Law of Giving and Receiving

> *Be unselfish. That is the first and final commandment for those who would be useful and happy in their usefulness. If you think of yourself only, you cannot develop because you are choking the course of development, which is spiritual expansion through thought for others.*
>
> —Charles W. Eliot

A genuine act of extending your hand to assist those who could use your help is selfless. Giving is a picturesque tale of bestowing acts of generosity upon others without regard for how you might benefit. Having compassion is a blessing in itself. Everything that we own comes from God, so who are we not to share? When we depart from this life, we cannot take anything with us except the contents of our heart. Giving to people isn't solely about fulfilling the obligations of your religion. When you act from the depths of your soul, the focus is placed on your thoughts, your stewardship, how you embrace the spirit of giving, and your dedication to meeting every call with the same compassion and determination to help elevate people to a better place.

Never pass up an opportunity to give, for in such generosity there lies precious lessons of empathy, kindness, a sincere desire to alleviate suffering, and a yearning to witness the smiles on people's faces. All of which requires sensitivity and an ability to give in a spirit of love. Why is it important to practice giving? Well, if you are one who gives without having secret ambitions or an appetite for praise, then you must realize how special it feels to give as if you have inexhaustible supplies. If you do not know the joy of devoting your time to those who are in need, or of giving for no other reason than feeling a sense of duty, maybe your heart has been conditioned to ignore the fact that such generosity tends to multiply in favor of those who bestow more than those who receive. Giving is so much more than the offering of materialistic valuables. Jesus taught the people, "Give, and it shall be given unto you." Anyone can give things away, but to do so with a fulfilled heart and gratitude makes the difference.

Volunteering is an excellent way to experience how rewarding it is to give to others. Visit an orphanage, a children's hospital, or the Salvation Army to become familiar with the spirit of giving your time and developing awareness for what a walk in someone else's shoes may be like.

Giving without expectation of receiving something in return will help make the world a brighter place. You could be a mentor or a tutor. The fact that you've extended your hand to assist people will make your heart stronger. Don't you dare worry about being ridiculed by those who are coldhearted. They act snobbish because they are full of discontent and hatred. Obviously, they lack the compassion to help people who are in need of a delicate hand and nonjudgmental boost.

Occasionally, while being a good steward, we may be confronted by folks who feel inclined to take advantage of our generosity. Should you feel as if you are being used or others are not genuinely appreciative for what you've done for them, don't allow their ignorance to change you. When we stop satisfying God's call and begin allowing others' actions to affect us, eventually it will alter the content of our heart forever.

Jewel

Give until your heart is satisfied.

Lesson 42:

Request Favors Only When You Need To

> *One never forgets to acknowledge a favor, no matter how small.*
>
> **—Moral Teaching of the Omaha**

Before asking someone to do you a favor, consider whether you are truly in need. Favors require delicate forethought. Any request that holds the potential to lighten your load should never result in others feeling as though your *call* is burdensome. Times will arise when, out of desperation or a shortage of time, we'll ask certain people for a favor out of a sense of urgency, but it shouldn't come at the expense of stepping on someone's feet.

When requesting a favor, ask for something that's practical—be considerate of other people's time and resources. Your perception of what constitutes proper timing isn't necessarily the next person's reality. Good people seldom take issue with lending a hand to help those in need; however, when their generosity becomes susceptible to usury, they will find a way to avoid you.

There's a flip side to this coin. It warns us to be watchful of those who may try to abuse our helpfulness under the guise of requesting a *favor*. Some people will ask you to do things such as lend them money, watch their children, or help with a task because they know you have a giving heart. There's no need to search their character for intent. Just be sure that when you honor a favor, the recipient is mindful that life is reciprocal. It has been said that birds of a feather flock together. Be aware of who you allow within your circle. There is an obvious distinction between those who mean you well and those who mean you no good!

No matter what, when doing someone a favor it should come from a sincere place in your heart. Dismiss the urge to remind people of what you've done for them. Such an offensive expression has the potential to negate your blessings. It may also insinuate that you have been expecting some type of recognition for your actions. Basically, what you pretended to have done from the kindness of your heart, will turn out to be disingenuous. A genuinely good deed always comes from a place deep within, where there is no estimation in helping others win.

Try to commit this to your memory: Every good deed is well documented. This is one of the beauties of doing things from the kindness of our heart. Absent tendencies to verbalize our moments of generosity, someone, somewhere is always keeping a tab on what we say and what we do!

> Be considerate when asking for a favor.
>
> —Michael T. Crawford

Lesson 43:

It's Cool to Be Brainy

> *The wise person who ceases to learn ceases to be wise.*
>
> **—African proverb**

Absent a hunger to challenge ourselves daily, we shouldn't expect to make it very far. We must develop a sincere love for pursuing knowledge that could help enhance the faculties of our mind. Too much television or playing video games is not good for our creative abilities. It obstructs the roads of possibilities by creating false adventures that are intangible in a world of fantasy. Furthermore, indulging in them too much can cause us to become lazy. If watching TV is a must, watch programs that have an educational value: *Brain Games, National Geographic, Jeopardy*, etc.

Constantly explore new ways to expand your creative thoughts. Contemplate the proverbs of different cultures. Study mathematics, science, history, and psychiatry. Never shy away from learning all you can about yourself. Study until your heart is content. Life will handsomely reward those who can demonstrate mental efficiency. Such is the window of opportunity that will provide you with a chance to become a doctor, lawyer, social worker, or banker. So the next time you are taunted because you enjoy being a bookworm, smile in the face of ignorance. For it is only through your diligent studying and unrelenting quest for seeking knowledge will you come to know the true power of your brilliancy.

Unquestionably, studying can be tedious. But what better way to spend your time than quietly engrossed in a book that can teach you something of great value? The more you read, the sharper your thinking abilities will become. Cultivation of our mind is the key to advancing in life. If we are to make the best of opportunities that await us, we must first learn where to find the information we need, and then, how to apply it. Have confidence in yourself. There is nothing to be afraid of except understanding the depth of your personal ignorance. In life anything is possible, but you must be prepared to work your plans and see them through without giving up. Nothing comes to a quitter except ridicule from choosing to be a failure.

Your creative abilities should never be wasted, and no idea should be left unexplored. Wisdom should never go unheeded. Take pride in learning how information can help elevate your state of mind. Try to study a variety of things that can provide you with an advantage.

It's cool to be a brain. Would you prefer to be a student of wisdom, or a performer of ignorance? How embarrassing to be quizzed and then fail for not knowing some of life's most fundamental facts. Do not let the joke be on you. The sham will not reveal itself until you show an unwillingness to seek mental cultivation. Read, study hard, pay attention, and most of all, never neglect to apply what you have learned.

Jewel

> What is life without a willingness to at least apply some of the things you have learned?
>
> —Anye Crawford

Lesson 44:

To Win You Must Be Persistent

> There is in this world no such force as the force of a man determined to rise.
>
> —W.E.B. DuBois

No one ever said life would be easy. Every person throughout the annals of history has been met with intimidating obstacles. But regardless of how they felt or what they had seen, they continued to press on. Who are we to give up so easily? Persistence is about having the willpower and a desire to follow through in all your missions despite opposition or fear of failing! Look around you. Every day people can be seen carelessly throwing their towel in before giving themselves an honest chance to succeed. It appears as if shedding tears over what they *think* they cannot do is preferable to defeating what's believed to be unconquerable. There are many things in life that are difficult, but how can you make it look easy if you lack a desire to go head-to-head with the problem?

There will be people who will be a distraction or attempt to persuade you to abandon your goals. Such pressure is indicative of the weakness that is common in a lot of people. If only they would try, they would realize how easily a lack of persistence can be conquered. Never worry about the people who seem disinterested in climbing the rungs of success. You must stay focused, think, and continue tabulating the moves you must make before you can arrive at the steps of your accomplishments. When we think of achieving that which we are aiming for, we must be engulfed by a burning desire, a desire to prevail. Execute your plans despite the hardships you encounter.

Do not be intimidated by thoughts of failing. Surround yourself with smart people who will encourage you to hold your head up high and keep going. Even if you finish last, keep going! Put it in your mind that you are a winner, and no matter who or what may get in your way, you possess the ability to keep fighting until you're declared victorious. Once you start something, turning back shouldn't be an option. Why would you want to? Does the prospect of clashing with difficulties frighten you? It shouldn't. Always put forth your best effort to complete whatever you have set your mind on. If at first you don't succeed, try again and again and again until at last you succeed. If your initial plan fails to bear fruit, do not hesitate to try something different. Ask for help and never let it be said that you had a habit of blaming others for your failures.

Do not judge me by my successes; judge me by how many times I fell and got back up again.

—Nelson Mandela

Lesson 45:

It's Impossible to Win Every Battle!

> *It is unlikely you will win ever battle, but if you choose wisely which battles are worth fighting, triumph will reveal itself.*
>
> **—Unknown**

No two battles are the same. Some will require a deployment of troops, while others necessitate nothing more than a touch of tactfulness. However, before we can determine which tactics to utilize or how best to respond to hostile actions and provocations, we must first calm our emotions and then study the problem. Regardless of who's involved, a conflict can be resolved or amplified way before it is exposed to the light of day. A true warrior doesn't react to raw emotions. Through self-discipline he or she will not impulsively become offended, nor initiate confrontations due to an inability to own up to their mistakes. Battles from within require being quick to think amid dark emotions, and possessing the willpower to patiently listen to opposing parties without being judgmental.

While the idea of self-preservation is indeed humanistic, there is a difference between acting in a way that insures one's continued survival and behaving in a way that's self-destructive.

Always choose your battles wisely. Before waging war on others, you must first have the courage to look in the mirror and assess your own flaws. And then, if you still believe that your position is appropriate, by all means, allow your truths and beliefs to lead the way. Do not emulate those who erroneously think that lashing out in anger is the best tactic for getting your point across. A fool rarely sees the errors of their ways.

Battles consist of taking a stand for a cause. Never be afraid to intelligently verbalize a valid concern, regardless of whether the concern is about injustice to you or others. Some people become emotionally and verbally paralyzed at the mere thought of taking a stand to be counted among real men and women who have lived their lives by passionately speaking against all odds. When you fight, be certain that it is a just fight. Whether you agree or not, people—great people—have sacrificed their lives so that one day we can all have a chance to reflect on the experiences and struggles of those who chose their battles wisely. God gave us a mouth to speak. Respectfully exert your opinion, demonstrate your ability to lead with a creative touch, and watch how you naturally prevail in any situation that arrives at your doorstep.

Do not allow your ethical compass to become corrupted due to the mocking of those who are weak-minded. Without a vigilant heart, very few people will have anything worthy to contribute except for complaints and an unwillingness to do anything to make the situation better. You are not a doormat, for if you were, humanity would never pass by an opportunity to wipe her feet on you.

Make no mistake about it, the world loves a champion; those who display courage while in the face of adversities. But it will always frown upon those who act irrationally. Stand tall when choosing your battles. You are men and women with dignity, self-respect, and layered principles that are uncompromising. Openly welcome folks to step up and be heard. There should never be a biased stench to your equality for all; to be equally just is our resolve. It shall forever permit us to avow our individuality, emotional discipline, and the welcoming of healthy debate.

Jewel

> *An argument is never a just response to a misunderstanding. Be careful how you interpret people's frustrations.*
>
> —Salimah Youngblood

Lesson 46:

The Obligations of Being Responsible

> *It is easy to dodge responsibilities, but we cannot dodge the consequences of dodging our responsibilities.*
>
> —Josiah Charles Stamp

Maturity—being reliable, sensible, or carrying yourself in a manner that projects an old soul. Those are hallmarks of someone who's capable of embracing responsibilities. When those who know a few things about accountability call upon you to assume specific duties, or invite you aboard to help manage a business, humbly smile with appreciation for recognition of your savvy. You were handpicked because someone felt confident that they could depend on you to tackle issues responsibly and delegate tasks to qualified individuals. Yes, you! A thinker who moves through life having made a personal pledge to do your best every day.

Sometimes when we have made it to the top and reflect on our trials and errors, it can feel surreal. Having confidence in your skills to get things done effectively is one thing, but to experience the trust others have placed in your ability to execute certain duties is an amazing experience. This is the type of harmonious sensibility that every soul needs to thrive with a valued smile. At times being responsible can be exhausting, but it is not a trait we can afford to live without. Responsibilities help strengthen our character. They prepare us to become effective leaders who cannot wait to blaze new trails. Stated briefly, responsibilities are what teach us the importance of being dedicated and never being a quitter.

There are other conveniences in this apartment, but the most important thing is to demonstrate that you are a responsible person. Take the initiative to assign tasks to those best suited to handle certain jobs. Always be on time. Very few people will provide you with an additional chance to prove your worth after it becomes evident that you are not dependable.

The Obligations of Being Responsible

Plenty of good-hearted folks have opened the doors of their homes to a friend who turned out to be very irresponsible and, ultimately, the cause of them losing a lot more than a valuable friendship.

Being responsible means you have a duty to step up and help bring the best out of others. Life doesn't consist solely upon your personal whims. Sometimes you'll have to demonstrate your compassion through providing others with an inspirational touch that can help them realize their personal competence.

> *Special people do things for the greater good.*
>
> —Xiomara B. Mulligan

If we expect to be taken seriously, we must show a consistent pattern for being responsible. Starting today, you have an obligation to inspire those around you to dig deep within themselves to come up with their brightest thoughts; thoughts that are original yet stimulating; thoughts which give way to inspirational hunches; thoughts that yearn for at least one chance to become acquainted with a desire to transform the intangible into a beautiful reality. Do you not see the picture? The more responsible we are, the greater our opportunities will be. Everyone will not be made of what you possess, but if you are capable of inspiring them, and showing them how to capitalize on their missteps, that will certainly be enough to afford them with the *mettle* to pursue their dreams.

> *It is better to be known as a responsible man or woman, than to be considered one who is constantly in need of instructions.*
>
> —Sharon Rogers

Lesson 47:

The Uncertainty of Gambling

> *After gambling away everything that you have worked so hard to obtain, the next to go is inheritance from a loved one.*
>
> —Derrick L. Crawford

Gambling is a very troubling road to travel down. It is one that leads directly to poverty. Why would you want to continuously waste your time and hard-earned money on such an uneven risk that could possibly leave you with nothing? It doesn't sound like a decision someone wise would make.

This is the dilemma: Initially, gambling appears to

be fun and lucrative. The first win creates excitement, an enticement for how easy it is to make quick money. After your second, third, or fourth win, you'll find yourself chasing after something that looks very promising. You may even believe you're creating a success story for yourself: but the foundation that you are building on is fragile.

Reflect on yourself for a bit. In your desperation for another chance to hit your next lick, you'll often find the following four factors: 1) You have ambition. The desire for procuring your next win is strong, almost with a sense of urgency to it. Nothing will be able to deter you from it. It's already fixed in your mind that you'll win and that's exactly what you intend on doing. 2) You are a visionary. You're able to clearly envision yourself lining up your ducks and creating a plan for selling each of them, for top dollar. 3) You own taking the initiative. No one has to tell you where to go for the best chance to triple your money. You will find it on your own. And last but not least, 4) You are a big dreamer. In your mind you've been convinced that to win big, you'll have to gamble big. But along with big gambles come huge losses. And the bigger you lose, the harder you will try to recoup what had only been obtained by mere chance in the first place.

What happens when you look around and see

you're all alone and flat broke? What's the next excuse for why you must sell your possessions? I'll tell you how it'll play out! You will cause yourself to suffer great humiliation. Remember when you were close to becoming a success? Now you'll be somewhere begging for a handout.

That one gamble that you were so convinced would place you back where you needed to be will be the nail in your coffin. Then what would our advice be good for? How different are you in comparison to a person who's a drug addict in search of their next fix? A disease is just that, a disease, and now it becomes your turn to attempt to care for the rehabilitation of your addiction, one day at a time. How sad it will be to see that you have wasted your precious talents on a vice that may lead to mental illness.

Why would anyone intelligent risk incurring debt, destroying valuable relationships, and agonizing over the dwindling of their wealth? It's bound to happen. That first chase will unquestionably lead to many more. Forget about the false promises you spew about being able to quit whenever you want, or being done after you get that one big win. News flash! By then you won't have the discipline to stop. You will always find hope in the prospect of that next lick. Common sense should tell you that it isn't logical to think it's possible to accumulate riches while entertaining a gambling habit. Stay away from games of chance or risk losing everything that has value and significance to you—it just might cost you the comforts of your family!

Your life is worth more than a gamble.

—John S. Ballard

Lesson 48:

The Accumulation of Wealth

> *If you keep your pockets full of coins, you will always have small change.*
>
> **—Yoruba proverb**

If we are to pursue any facet of prosperity, it must first begin with our state of mind. Anyone who has become rich or accumulated wealth was first prosperous mentally and spiritually. At some point soon, it would serve us well to seek the counsel of those who have successfully made it to the top. Ask a question if you must, but the key will be to listen well. Keep an open mind and be willing to accept sound advice. Under no circumstances should you mingle with those who are unwilling to look beyond today. Their unproductive views can become contagious.

To accumulate wealth, we must have a definitive plan, sound ideas and an imagination that fosters big dreams. Become an example of your desires. Question: Are you in an environment that can help nurture your aspirations? Are you receptive to mental currents? Meaning—can you build upon the ideas of those who have a creative mind?

Our thoughts of securing wealth cannot advance if we don't have a purpose for wanting the money. Do not be like the kid in the candy store who cannot make up his mind, and so he loses himself by having an excited urge to sample some of everything which appeals to him. Focus. Know with great certainty exactly what it is that you want. Without a dominant vision, all your thoughts for accumulating wealth will be wishful thinking.

If a philanthropist were to provide you with one million dollars today, it would probably ruin you. Those who are old acquaintances of wealth understand the respect that must be given to money. Cash is a necessary medium that's utilized for the purpose of attaining and financing things that are required to help advance our goals. The true purpose of money is to make it work for you!

The average person comes across a few pennies and immediately goes crazy, purchasing things they have no real use for. When the money is gone, they are right back to entertaining impoverished ways and basking in thoughts of misery. When you had money, you didn't know what to do with it. There is an old saying, "A fool and his money are soon parted." With a disposition for becoming wealthy comes refinement, style, and an ability to understand the value of being a thinker. By all means, be yourself, but show the world you are savvy enough to evolve with your thoughts in a creative way.

After you have successfully made it, be sure to return to help lift others from their burdensome conditions. You won't be able to help anyone until you learn how to help yourself. What would be the true meaning of your values if you didn't return for those who have always been by your side, but just didn't understand the potential of their mind? Show them! I am certain that if you were doing anything contrary to your moral obligations, it would constitute an act of prejudice; so accumulate money with a heart that will find a way to extend a hand to the less fortunate.

Do you honestly need to be reminded? Your deeds should be positive. Do not sit someplace utilizing your creativity to conjure up get-rich-quick schemes. They will never pay off. Visualization, courage, persistence, and perfection reward handsomely. The laws of prosperity will work in your favor if you act accordingly. You've been given the basics, now go out and seek.

Whatever profession you choose, stick to it. Learn the ins and outs of your craft with confidence for what you are doing. Think in abundance and that is exactly what you will receive. Stop being a consumer. Try your hand at becoming a producer for a change.

Jewel

> *The trick is to become money conscious, and surround yourself with those who understand the importance of making money work for them.*
>
> **—Kevin Smalls**

Lesson 49:

The Exaggeration of Arrogance

> *A person who is offensively full of pride and arrogance cannot see the flaws of their own faults.*
>
> **—Raymond Powell**

Arrogance, oh yes! It is an attitude that will create a strong distaste towards you as a person. Please explain, what excuse could be offered as to why you have an arrogant disposition towards people? What makes your story—triumphs or misfortunes—so much better than anyone else's? Your overly inflated sense of superiority is unreasonable. Your constant desire to highlight the faults of those around you is unconscionable. Your poorly chosen words and bad manners do nothing more than create ill-feelings and a prayer for you to miraculously disappear.

It is you who secretly despises the pleasantness of life for no apparent reason. No wonder it's difficult for you to detect at least one honorable quality within yourself. Your craziness will remain exactly what it is if you persist with thinking that you're God's gift to humanity. Why? Because you seem to be preoccupied with dealing with false pride and refuse to take a long, hard look at yourself with the intentions of correcting your flaws.

Happiness is hard to find when we spend so much time being belligerent, acting self-righteous, and contemptuously walking around, looking down on other people who in their own right are truly remarkable folks. Who appointed you or me to search for chinks in the armor of others? It is our attitude that is the sole culprit for our failures in life. Having a nasty ego decreases the probability of someday having an abundance of joyous prosperity. Get rid of the chip on your shoulder, learn to be modest and maybe, just maybe, you will have a real chance to become someone decent!

The Exaggeration of Arrogance

Stop thinking it's cool to go around pretending to be something that only exists as a figment of your imagination.

—Jermaine Jones

Lesson 50:

Be Thankful for Your Talents

> *Let not what you cannot do tear from your hands what you can.*
>
> **—Ashanti proverb**

You possess the ability to do anything your heart desires. There is absolutely nothing in this world that is impossible to accomplish, if you put your mind to it. Should you begin entertaining thoughts of not being able to do something, you will have already failed. Yesterday, opportunities may have been limited, but today they can literally be found around every corner, if only you would search. When you have learned to think and formulate solid ideas, the world will become more receptive to you. And, because of your ability to apply what you know, life will provide you with a glimpse of the immutable laws that regulate our lives.

To prevent falling behind due to atrophying abilities, it's important to be consistent with our concepts. As times change, so should our abilities. What may have been considered brilliant today may become irrelevant tomorrow, with forgotten recognition for our originality.

Try to always maintain a deep belief in what you can do. The laws of nature are in your favor. When demonstrating the ability to work in conjunction with the natural order of things rather than against them, things will flow more fluidly. When we go against such a delicate balance it tends to create worries, frustration, bitterness, jealousy, unnecessary problems, and everything that's considered debilitating. No wonder it appears to be difficult to get a grip while trying to climb out of the barrel of crabs.

When you come up with bold ideas, try to create a strong desire for transforming your visions into reality. Not only will your approach provide you with confidence, it will also motivate you to find ways to help bring your creativity to fruition. Every new day awaits us with a multitude of possibilities. All that is required of *us* is to be mentally, physically, and emotionally prepared to explore what just might turn out to be the greatest contribution to humankind. Until we do so, it will be extremely challenging to place ourselves in a position that grants us permission to forge an inspiring mark. Remain patient. In due time, all good things will come your way. Nothing worth admiration will occur when we would like it to. Do your best work by striving diligently and never taking your eyes off of your objective. If you keep those jewels in the front of your mind, each day, your abilities will improve.

Remember: just because you're capable of doing something better than someone else, it doesn't give you the right to be a show-off. It is unbecoming to flaunt our talents in the face of those who have yet to ripen. You know better than anyone else what you can do when you apply yourself. That should serve as a reminder to be modest. An eagerness to gloat about what you can do will turn genuine people against you. Those who are truly talented only speak of their ingenuity when it's absolutely necessary. If you place all of your abilities on the table today, tomorrow you will not have anything left that may be of use. Always try to keep something in reserve.

By the conclusion of this book, you will have been

offered many priceless jewels, but none will be worth their weight if you are unwilling to apply what you've learned and share them with someone who might be in a similar position as the one you were once in.

Jewel

> When we have learned how to value our talents, all sorts of opportunities will suddenly appear.

Lesson 51:

The Graciousness of Integrity

> *In all your official acts, self-interest shall be cast aside. You shall look and listen to the welfare of the people and have always in view, not only the present, but the coming generations—the unborn of the future nation.*
>
> —Dekawidah

Integrity: consistency in the structure of your honor, your unwavering principles, and the sparkling righteousness of your character. Being a person of integrity provides you with protection against the negative influence of pettiness that has become the norm. We must live by unbendable standards that cannot be compromised for any reason. Let there never be a price or temptation of any kind that can entice you to transgress the boundaries of what you know to be correct.

In the moments when we are not quite ourselves, it is easy to become entangled in the emotions of those who find themselves in desperate situations. Protect yourself at all costs against the propositions of those who pretend to have your best interests at heart, for such interests will never be beneficial. Not every smile is inspired by true happiness. Abandoning your integrity is a betrayal to your character and there is no one to blame except for the person you see in the mirror. We know better, and when we know better, we're supposed to do better! The smooth voice in our head is always trying to warn us against doing foolish things, talking out of turn, and violating the rights of others, yet we pay it no mind. Why is that?

The quality of your character can only be measured by your undying determination to keep your integrity intact, regardless of who may be around. When temptation knocks on your door, and it will, do not compromise the structure of your values. Have a little bit of class!

How will you know if you have integrity? Well, you should be able to answer that question by acknowledging whether you are 100 percent truthful with yourself as well as others. Do you stand for something that unequivocally represents the strength of your character? Who will feel confident in trusting us if we have a history of exhibiting weakness? The annals of history are replete with lessons of those who were tempted to do the wrong thing. What is done under the cover of night will be revealed in the light, even if it takes a while before it has been discovered.

If we walk with truth in our hearts, we shall never go astray. Do not worry about what other people think of you. There will always be someone envious of you. All that should concern you is your ability to listen to your inner voice, the one that nags you to do the right thing.

A person who can honor their integrity is bound to become morally wealthy.

—Quimyll Ballard

Lesson 52:

Big Egos Hinder Our Mental Growth

> *You must be free of ego when you are with others, so expand your heart, be courteous, cooperative, and loving.*
>
> —Shih Cheng Yen

Has anyone ever suggested that you may be a bit overly fascinated with yourself? Do you spend an excessive amount of time trying to convince others that you are more than what they see? A constant attempt to be validated could be a sign of a deep-rooted problem. Those who have hawkish egos seldom consider themselves to be a spoke in the wheel. Instead, in their mind, they are and will always be the hub. In the eyes of such people, the world is a chessboard, upon which everyone else is a pawn to be strategically positioned at his or her whim. Make no mistake about it, folks with abnormal egos believe they are entitled to whatever their heart desires! What a shallow way to live. Unless we are suffering from a mental health disorder, it is difficult to function with exaggerated thoughts of ourselves and others. As we grow older our way of thinking becomes more warped. Initially we have a fixed opinion about everything, and soon there becomes little or no chance for correcting our flaws.

Those who have insatiable egos tend to operate in secrecy. Having a false sense of superiority, they are constantly lurking around, sizing people up to take advantage of them. They will never accept responsibility for their actions unless they are caught red-handed. And even then, they will cast blame on someone other than themselves. If these shoes appear to fit your feet, I pose the question—who are you to rudely speak as if you know something about everything? Silently you laugh in amusement at the misfortunes and perceived ignorance of others. Are your thoughts truly what you believe, or can it be that you are mentally unbalanced and lack an ability to see how you are uncompromising and extremely antagonistic?

One of the most unfortunate things about the ego is, it will not offer you a positive reason to get to know a person before hastily forming an opinion about whether they are worth getting to know better. Right away the ego will create shallow reasons why a particular person isn't good enough: "He acts weak," or "She talks funny," or "He looks like a nut," or "She acts too weird." The ego is only concerned with the importance of its own perceptions. It constantly perceives things that may be possible, yet highly unlikely. Why? Your perception of life isn't someone else's reality; your likes and dislikes will differ from other people, and you must respect it.

A person who's endowed with humility does not entertain a false ego. You cannot consider yourself to be real if you carry yourself in a way that leads people to believe your thinking and emotions are corrupted. Everything isn't about you or me! You are not a victim, so don't act like one by blaming others for your mistakes. We all have obligations of some sort. That's just the way life is. There is never an appropriate excuse for overvaluing your actions, self-worth, or achievements.

When your ego begins to inflate, you've entered a very dangerous place; such is what occurs when the ego feels as if it's being attacked. An ability to turn our conscious thoughts off and a sense of being better than everyone else are signs of troubling disorders that are commonly found in those who enjoy masquerading as someone they are not. Find comfort in being yourself, not an egotistical person who operates from the extremities of their mind.

> *Refrain from being high and mighty, it may ultimately lead to your downfall.*
>
> **—Timothy Butler**

Lesson 53:

The Best Have Failed Innumerable Times

> *Your failure in life comes from not realizing your nearness to success when you give up.*
>
> **—Yoruba proverb**

"Ladies and gentlemen, welcome to the University of Hard Knocks!" I would like to talk about the misconceptions that we often have pertaining to *failure*. Failing shouldn't cause you to have an emotional breakdown. Many great people such as Thomas Edison, Booker T. Washington, Helen Keller, and Henry Ford temporarily agonized over coming up short of their mark, but they remained persistent until they finally prevailed. When failure strikes, it can be disheartening to witness your sacrifices and hard work go down the drain. Perhaps failure appeared due to you spending too much time over-thinking; maybe you have yet to discover the genius that awaits awakening; or it could be because you may have not devoted enough time to developing your ideas. If you remain steadfast, failure is only a temporary setback that provides us with a chance to reflect on our mistakes and then come back stronger with the capacity and wisdom to secure a win.

Resist the urge to become comfortable with the company of procrastination because it has vowed to continually test the resolve of everyone who has dreams of becoming great. Many of us have missed out on the gifts of life because we are of the mindset that the perfect timing has yet to arrive. There will never be a more appropriate time than the present. To become a winner, we must remain open-minded, courageous, and inspired by the thought of accomplishing our objectives, regardless of what you think you lack! Have faith in your abilities. God has your back, but *only* after you've proven to have faith in yourself.

It doesn't matter what position we occupy in life. Failure is necessary if we plan to become a success.

The Best Have Failed Innumerable Times

The ingredients in the lessons of failing are what we seek to learn. Respect and admiration are extended to the person who works through a problem as opposed to guessing what may have gone wrong. You are currently in a position that will help you recognize your errors. Be eager to move forward with intentions of accomplishing everything you have begun. Leave no stone unturned. If you pursue a certain course, make sure you complete it.

No, we should never expect to fail. There is plenty of evidence that suggests no one is ever labeled a failure until it becomes clear by way of their actions. When you meet failure, don't become so frustrated that you give up. Try again, again, and again. Those who are successful in life didn't become so because they allowed defeat to throw itself in the path of progress. Are you serious? You have knowledge and a very creative mind. What will you do with what you have? You have an appetite to continue pressing on. Where are you headed? You have a strong desire to leave your mark on this world. And now is the perfect time to be an example to everyone who determined a long time ago that you wouldn't amount to anything worth a second thought. Silly people! When you're not afraid to fail, you will suddenly discover how powerful your thoughts can be.

The quality of your work is a definitive reflection of your thoughts. Let every task that you set out to accomplish have a meaningful purpose. Be neat, remain ambitious and constantly seek counsel from the wise to make sure your plan has the best chance of becoming a story that can meet the test of time. If you dedicate yourself to perfecting this advice, you will never be labeled a failure.

Jewel

> *The wisdom of failure will only reveal itself to those who are inspired by the thought of knowing they are that much closer to meeting success.*
>
> —Barbara Rachet

Lesson 54:

Don't Act Small-Mindedly

> Snatch a little measly advantage and miss the big one.
>
> —Anderson

While on your journey you may only bump into a few people who will reciprocate your philanthropic gestures. A lot of folks pretend to do things in a bighearted way, but if the truth be told, their spirit has been plagued by a petty nature. Such individuals tend to create molehills out of situations that warrant absolutely no energy at all. Try bringing them into a constructive conversation and you'll quickly discover how little they have to offer. Why? Because for some odd reason, small-minded people believe everything revolves around them. They are self-centered, petty, loud, manipulative, and untrustworthy. At all times, you must keep them at a safe distance or be prepared to compromise your peace of mind and your ability to judge wisely.

Usury and pettiness go hand-in-hand. If you can spot one, expect the other to be nearby. Stay on point. People will come to you with the ability to obtain just about anything they want. Yet, they will abuse your generosity to get more of what their greedy heart desires. See, when you live life being petty, every thought is about me, me, me! You will encounter, "What's in it for me?" or "Can you give me some more?" or "What can you do for me?" There's never enough of anything for someone who is petty. They'll always come around with their hand out, and if you owe them even ten cents, they will be certain to cry about every penny of it. Being small-minded will cause you to complain about everything.

Whenever you encounter people who are small-minded, you're looking at clowns who have a false sense of themselves. When they're in need, your door will be the first they come knocking on. Though you did nothing wrong, charge their actions to the attraction of your character. Parasites have a way of knowing who provides without a concern for ampleness. But should a time arise when there's an urgency to summon them for help, they will never treat you with the same compassion that you treated them with. Their help will be superficial and consist of scraps that are hardly befitting for anyone with a heart of gold!

Take your time and give plenty of thought to your need to accept things from people who are small-minded and petty. Surely they, too, deserve blessings, but certainly not at the expense of a secret clause that comes attached to their deeds.

> *The best way to slay a small-minded dragon is by giving it a glass of water to extinguish its dangerous fire.*
>
> **—John S. Ballard**

Lesson 55:

It's Time for Change

> *It takes a deep commitment to change and an even deeper commitment to grow.*
>
> —Ralph Emerson

No one ever enjoys the certainty of change. It can be uncomfortable and outright scary at times. However, for those of us who live life perpetually, nourishing criminal tendencies, change is a matter of life and death. Take a moment to hit your pause button. Sit back and relax. Now, without seeking to blame anyone else for your actions, I would like for you to think about the amount of time you spend every day daydreaming about ways to *attempt* to get over on people. Looking at yourself in the mirror is one of the hardest things to do. Nobody wants to acknowledge having a flawed character, nor errors in their thinking. But we do, and so we must address the issue of changing our ways in order to become responsible people.

Change is a process that will take a lot of mental strength and the courage to check yourself way before someone else has to. Because our thinking patterns—lack of empathy, blaming others for our actions, acting as if we are so unique, and having an inability to grasp how our actions injure other people—have caused us to adopt a radical view of the world, changing will not be easy. When we have reached a certain point in life and have determined that we have been our own worst enemy, then we can proceed to the next level. The behavior and thinking patterns of a criminal are no different than that of an alcoholic or drug addict.

Only two things are promised to a criminal: death or a lengthy prison sentence. To elude either of them, we must change the way we respond to negative thoughts. Change will require us to be vigilant of our thoughts and actions. Don't just recognize your poor thinking patterns, analyze them! Today, start considering the possible consequences of your actions. Maybe it's the humiliation of being arrested, or of spending long periods of time away from those you love, or of being controlled by other people, that will serve as a reminder for you to do the right thing.

Thoughts do not become consequential until we act upon them. To be a good thinker, you must observe your thoughts all the time. Do not wait until after you have done something foolish to ask yourself these wise questions: "What was I thinking?" or "Why did I decide to drive home after having so many drinks?" It will have become too late. Before the commission of any criminal act, there will always be a thought. If we change the way we think, we can prevent ourselves from suffering the repercussions later.

Unless and until we are willing to explore new thoughts, new feelings, or new ways of doing things, there's a chance that we'll continue to miss out on circumstances that have the potential to be life-altering. Demonstrating a willingness to change shows actual growth, courage, and confidence in your abilities. On a daily basis we have many things going on, so sometimes it becomes difficult to remember the importance of frequently making time for self-reflection in order to evaluate whether there's something within that we need to tweak.

Always make time before you go to sleep to rewind the tapes of your day. Review how you carried yourself; how you spoke to people; and most importantly, what type of thoughts did you entertain? If you fall short of having been positive, make adjustments to correct your weaknesses. Act before it becomes too late. Be mindful. Step outside of your comfort zone and be completely honest about the thoughts you're entertaining as well as your feelings. You will go far if you're truthful about the adjustments you need to make.

Jewel

> *Change is a natural occurrence. Welcome it and witness how much better things become.*

Lesson 56:

Be a Good Judge of Character

> *The value of a man should be seen in what he gives and not what he is able to receive.*
>
> —Albert Einstein

"The youth have many wonderful things to be inspired by," a wise woman said. Because you possess so many enlightening jewels, your ability to accurately assess those who may be good for your mental growth is often a telltale sign of whether you are a good judge of character. It is not safe to embrace or confide in people solely because they take an interest in you, or because a friend introduces an acquaintance, leaving you to feel obligated to accommodate them. You should never be in a hurry to think that other people will possess your insight, common sense, or moral decency. Patience and mental growth do not happen overnight. As with the preparation of any delightful meal, it takes time.

Consistency in your thinking and good deeds are the keys to living a responsible life. We should walk our journey in search of the good in others, but we must be aware of those who do not mean us any good. Regardless of how many times you give them the benefit of the doubt, they will continuously disappoint you; then befriend you, due to hidden agendas. Take time to investigate the hearts of those who are new to you. Not in a paranoid way, but in a sense of optimism. Judge correctly and you will rarely choose a companion who's burdensome.

Whether meeting people on your own time or through business dealings, be an excellent judge of character. Try to make it a golden rule to never introduce someone you haven't known for a while to your trusted friends. Nowadays, people are seldom who they say they are. Besides, a friend should never have to pay the price if a stranger turns out to be a living nightmare.

> *The only person who never makes a mistake is the one who never does anything wrong.*
>
> **— Raymond Powell**

Lesson 57:

Imposing on Others Isn't Good

> *There isn't anything noble about being superior to another person. True nobility is in being superior to the person you once were.*
>
> **—Unknown**

Having knowledge of self, and knowing what you stand for, can prevent others from imposing on you. When we mingle with the wrong people, they tend to believe we are inferior, impressionable, and easily intimidated. As a result, they will attempt to persuade you to do things that will never be in your best interest. Sometimes they will even try using a more subtle approach, in which case you won't always be able to immediately recognize their angle, or see the obstacles they intentionally place in your way. In time, you will come to learn that those who impose on others are the same people whose sole goal is to manipulate situations and the people around them, so every outcome works to their advantage.

Due to spitefulness, jealousy, or an inclination to hold onto valuable positions, folks will try imposing their will on you in hopes of hindering you from making progress. Do not allow such people to distract you; stay focused and keep your eyes on the prize. Now is the perfect time to be conscious of your actions. Make sure that you never submit to anything that goes against your mental growth and development.

Here's something that can benefit you: Anyone who claims to respect you would never try to impose their will on you. You have a very strong mind with the faculty to think and create just as well as, if not better than, those who occupy positions of power. There is no reason why you should find yourself at the bottom, looking up to those who have created a way to impose their economic status, way of thinking, or religion upon you. We have all been created with the intellect to become the most powerful person in the world,

Imposing on Others Isn't Good

if only we are willing to put forth the effort to fully apply ourselves with complete faith in our abilities.

Stand on your own two feet and stop allowing others to impose their will on you. You can fumble, walk into a brick wall, or crash and burn without the assistance of someone who is unable to think as well as you. I'm sure we all know someone who cannot follow instructions, or who's incapable of recognizing the dangers that sometimes lie in the road ahead. Try not to become the person who constantly finds themselves missing out on everything good because they were led in a direction that served no purpose whatsoever.

Listen, it's completely up to you whether you'll choose to do for self, or forever be subjected to the whims of others. It's time for us to get our act together and stop making excuses for our inability to do what we should have done a long time ago.

Always be a thinker. Don't be a puppet on a string for anyone!

Lesson 58:

Use Your Head for Something Besides a Hat Rack

> *It is the tree that unhurriedly embraces its destiny that will grow to meet its fullest potential.*
>
> —Jamie L. Crawford

There are no fools residing on the top of the mountain, only wise folks who keep a watchful eye on a few rebellious wanderers walking below. Through our actions, speech, and mannerisms it will be determined how far we have come and how much farther we have yet to go. Everything we do from this day forward will be scrutinized. Each utterance will be searched for contradictions. Our manners will be combed for appropriateness, and our actions will be methodically explored for signs of uncorrected flaws. It wouldn't be that big of a deal if you lacked potential, but you, my friend, have an air about you that conveys greatness in the making. Now, a crowd has assembled in anticipation of witnessing whether you are who you say. Who else could you possibly be? Wise, disciplined, and creative; sounds like someone worthy of a closer inspection to me. Your experiences are what have enriched you. They are uniquely your own. Hold them close and realize that in their absence you may not be what you turned out to be. The knowledge you possess is still in its developmental stages. Have patience.

God did not create us to play the role of a clown. He took the time to fashion us in expectation that we might choose to seek knowledge that's consistent with the wisdom of those who came long before us. When we become discerning enough to grasp the depths of what we can become, then we will be permitted to come into our personal truth, a truth that is radiantly engulfed by uncommon wisdom.

It is considerably clever to surround yourself with people who have brilliant minds. Anyone can sit at a table with folks who think they know it all, but it is an honorable privilege to sit among men and women who have a deep passion for expressing their creative ideas. Be careful. You may not meet a lot of people who understand how to benefit from the ingenuity of a sage. The common person may sit in awe of the extraordinary abilities of the wise, and never consider asking a single question.

Jewel

> *A great truth sometimes appears so simple that it fails to make an impression, and therefore takes a long time to be realized.*
>
> **—Spanish proverb**

Lesson 59:

The Scorn of Prejudice

> *If my ambitions have been fueled by condemning people before gathering all of the facts, then what right do I have to call myself a just person?*
>
> —Re'Nee Taylor

I see the fear in your eyes. I hear the callousness in every word that you intentionally shoot with hopes of killing my creative spirit. I feel your persecutory vibrations, the ones that find comfort at the core of who you truly are. Nevertheless, I will continue to be who you know I am! Whether it is your sunless thoughts, or the grimacing expression upon your face, or the stench of animosity that unrelentingly seeps from your rotten glands, you should be aware that your flawed judgments have come full circle.

Although we are far from perfect, and haven't done so well with being communal, we still see you! We see the multitude of disparities that you have intentionally set in motion. We see how you arrogantly spread falsehoods in an attempt to vilify our character. We see how your unreasonable disposition creates hostile environments that foster ill-manners in people who don't know a thing about us. How delighted you must be. Question: *Is that not a form of prejudice?*

> There's none so blind as those who will not see.
>
> **—English proverb**

So, if everything you have read thus far is incorrect, then explain to me—why must you try so hard to blot out our monumental contributions to science, psychology, politics, mathematics, and at the very least, the construction of ancient civilizations, you know, the ones that flawlessly thrived way before the birth of what you insist was the beginning? It seems as if you have taken your perception of things literally. News flash! Your perception is not my reality. And this is in part what has brought us to the table today.

Always be just with people, regardless of what they may look like or how different they are from you. Prejudice limits the natural expansion of our heart and mind. As we become wiser, we will at some point reflect on circumstances, relationships and certain individuals who were biased towards us for no valid reason.

Don't allow people to degrade you. Regardless of what direction you travel in life, be sure to exemplify dignity when in the midst of those who are offensive. Walk with your head up high! Show the world that you are better than those who haven't been so good to you. No, it doesn't have anything to do with turning the other cheek. It simply means that you have elected to take the high road. By taking such an approach it offers the best chance for helping the ignorant reflect on the biases of their soul. When we maintain a positive attitude, it should serve as a reminder for us to be the best that we can be and to always treat other people with love and appreciation. Being prejudiced will stunt the growth of humanity. It will prevent all of us from collectively evolving as beautiful human beings. Life is a gift. It is for helping people to bring forth their best, not hinder them from becoming a beacon of inspiration.

Do not be so quick to judge. You don't know what the next person has been through. It is better to offer a helping hand as opposed to a foot on someone's neck. Keep in mind, our personal experiences and degrees of knowledge do not equate to the next person's reality. In other words, what you deem to be offensive may be something that someone else in their ignorance felt was okay to say.

> *Always be certain that the words people speak are truly what you believe them to be before you react. And should it call for a reaction, let it be one that is absent of a single drop of prejudice or malice in your heart.*
>
> **—La'Shanda Crawford**

> You can't change how people treat you or what they say about you. All you can do is change how you react to it.
>
> —Spanish proverb

Conclusion

I awoke this morning feeling excited to have completed another book. As I sat in predawn silence, contemplating the conclusion, it suddenly occurred to me that my talent for writing is a breath of fresh air to some, a welcoming light to those plagued by trying times, and a ray of hope for someone on the verge of giving up. *Traits and Emotions of a Salvageable Soul, Volume II* is a reminder of our genius, self-worth, and capabilities. When it was only an idea in my mind, I was hopeful that it could be a direct line of communication between my mind and yours. After the completion of *Volume I*, I felt obligated to creatively highlight our potential. God willing, I have done justice for the people who are in need the most. Everyone in this world doesn't have a shoulder to lean on, nor a voice of reason to encourage them to find a way to be their best.

Life isn't easy. Only after difficulty does ease appear. I didn't have to personally witness anyone struggling, I sensed it. And so, in an attempt to revitalize your spirit, I picked up my pencil and began writing in the hope that I could at least assist one person in finding their balance, overcome their fears, or rise to a new level, right amongst the stars.

It has been a privilege to be a steward of the people. Each day I have found myself more and more humbled. Knowledge belongs to no one, but we all have an obligation to share what we know, if someone is willing to listen and learn. PAY THE MESSAGE FORWARD.

Coming Soon: *Silenced by a Predator's Threat*

www.ingramcontent.com/pod-product-compliance
Lightning Source LLC
Chambersburg PA
CBHW070546010526
44118CB00012B/1239